# Simple Machine Sewing

## A BEGINNER'S GUIDE TO MAKING HOME ACCESSORIES, BAGS, CLOTHES, AND MORE

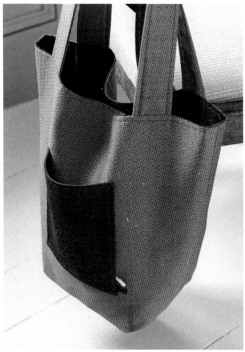

## ANGELA PRESSLEY

CICO BOOKS
LONDON  NEW YORK

To my children, Ez and Xanthe, I'm proud to say that the creative apple hasn't fallen far from the tree! x

Published in 2024 by CICO Books
An imprint of Ryland Peters & Small Ltd
20–21 Jockey's Fields         341 E 116th St
London WC1R 4BW         New York, NY 10029

www.rylandpeters.com

10 9 8 7 6 5 4 3 2 1

Text © Angela Pressley 2024
Design, illustration, and photography © CICO Books 2024
Sewing machine on page 115 provided by
Janome Corporation.

A CIP catalog record for this book is available from the Library of Congress and the British Library.

ISBN: 978 1 80065 294 1

Printed in China

Designer: Alison Fenton
Photographer: James Gardiner
Stylist: Nel Haynes
Illustrator: Cathy Brear
Editor: Jenny Dye
Art director: Sally Powell
Creative director: Leslie Harrington
Production manager: Gordana Simakovic
Publishing manager: Carmel Edmonds

FSC
www.fsc.org

MIX
Paper from
responsible sources
FSC® C106563

# Contents

Introduction 4
Sewing Kit 5

## Chapter 1

## Home Furnishings and Decorations 6

Napkins and Table Runner 8
Bowl and Mug Cozies 11
Zippered Pillow 14
Soft Plant Pot Covers 19
Pet Bed 22
Garden Kneeler 26
Pouffe 28
Seat Pad 31
French Press Jacket 34

## Chapter 2

## Accessories, Bags, and Purses 38

Scrunchie 40
Key Fob Wristlet 42
Reversible Notebook Cover 44
Cozy Slippers 47
Sleep Mask 50
Neck Tie 54
Bucket Hat 57
Reversible Tote Bag 60
Bag Strap 64
Foldable Coin Purse 66
Foldaway Tote 69
Glasses/Phone Case 72
Crossbody Bag 74
Plush Tote 78
Cosmetics Bag 82
Bag Organizer 88
Laptop Bag 92

## Chapter 3

## Garments 96

Cross-back Apron 98
Duster Jacket 101
Tailor-made Top 104
Drawstring Skirt 109

## Workshops

Workshop 1: Cutting Out and Pinning 112
Workshop 2: Sewing Skills 114
Workshop 3: Seams, Hems, Mitered Corners, and Darts 118
Workshop 4: Building on Your Skills 122
Workshop 5: Hand Sewing 124
Workshop 6: Patchwork and Quilting 126
Workshop 7: Bag-making Skills and Fastenings 128

Templates 132
Index, Suppliers, and Acknowledgments 144

# Introduction

Are you ready for an amazing sewing education? Everyone needs some sewing know-how in their lives. If you can sew, the possibilities are endless. You can choose to sew for charity, for profit, for environmental reasons, as a creative indulgence, to clothe your family, or just simply as an excuse to put your phone down.

Textiles are all around us, to see and to handle, but it is how they make us feel that is key. No doubt you will own sewn items that you have an emotional connection to, so why not be at the start of that journey by making your own special pieces?

Taking inspiration from my sewing classes over the years, I have crammed a storehouse of information into this book. You will gain confidence as you progress through the different levels and projects using instructions, methods, and shortcuts that are tried and tested.

I have raided my precious fabric stash for you, and I hope you like my choices! I've used modern, on-trend textiles such as natural fibers including Harris Tweed (for the Crossbody Bag on page 74) and linen (for the Napkins on page 8), tactile choices such as wool bouclé (for the Bucket Hat on page 57) and faux fur (for the Plush Tote on page 78), and vintage finds (for the Drawstring Skirt on page 109 and printed Table Runner on page 8). Enjoy searching for your fabrics, reuse and recycle what you already have, and give new life to treasured pieces.

The real way to sew in a sustainable way is not to worry about the grainline, pattern matching, fussy cutting, and getting the recommended fabric for the project you've seen. Ditch these ideas and sew your own path by using offcuts and remnants, and mixing different fabrics—you could even combine stretch with non-stretch if these are the fabrics you love and have to hand. The important thing is to fall in love with your fabric choices because they will get you to the end of the project.

I'll never forget the sense of accomplishment I felt when I finished my first skirt—I realized I could now sew things exactly the way I wanted them, and it opened up a whole new world for me. It will for you, too!
Happy sewing!
Angela x

## Before you begin

If you're new to sewing, or if you come across a technique you don't know, check out the workshops section on pages 112–131. Please note that all seam allowances are ⅜in (1cm) unless stated otherwise. Each project is marked with a skill level—start with projects that have a skill level of one star and then move on to projects that have a skill level of two or three stars once you have gained more experience. On some of the illustrations, you will see green and red colored dots that show you where to sew—see page 114 for the key.

# Sewing Kit

To get started, these are the tools you will need. You might find you already have some of these, so you may only need to add a few more.

## Basic sewing kit

Sewing machine—There are many different brands of sewing machines to choose from, each offering a wide range of stitch options. The stitches you will use the most are straight stitch and zigzag stitch, but other stitches are useful (see page 114). If purchasing a new machine, look for one that has a free arm and detachable feet. You'll find portable versions easier to set up and put away. Spending more may mean you have a stronger motor to tackle bag making and soft furnishings and an automatic buttonhole feature is always an advantage.

Sewing machine needles—Make sure you pick the right type for your machine, and remember, the lower the number, the thinner and finer the needle. Use a size 10/70 for delicate fabrics (such as the fabric for the Duster Jacket on page 101), size 14/90 for medium-weight fabrics such as quilting cottons (for the Bag Organizer on page 88) and size 16/100 for heavier fabrics like bouclé (for the Laptop Bag on page 92).

Pencil

Pen

Tailor's chalk

Ruler

Set square

Tape measure

Hem gauge

Graph paper/dot-and-cross paper—for making templates

Parchment/greaseproof paper for tracing templates

Scissors for cutting paper

Sharp scissors (about 9½in/24cm long) —kept especially for cutting fabric (using them for paper will make them blunt)

Small, pointed fabric scissors/thread snips

Plastic-headed pins

Fabric clips

Safety pins—ones with push-in plastic heads are ideal

Seam ripper

Hand sewing needles (sharps)

## Extra tools

These items are needed for some of the projects and are also useful to have in your sewing kit:

Pointer—for pushing out corners

Tailor's ham—see pressing on page 117

Seam roller—see pressing on page 117

Quilter's tape—see zipper technique on page 130

Walking foot—see quilting on page 126

Zipper foot (see page 130)

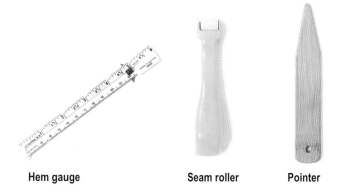

Hem gauge     Seam roller     Pointer

You will also need to start a collection of different materials and threads, so look out for these:

## Fabrics

I've really enjoyed putting the different fabrics together for the projects in this book. All the projects will work well with a medium weight non-stretch cotton (organic or recycled), also known as a quilting cotton or craft cotton, linen, hemp, or bamboo. For the clothing projects you can opt for more flowing fabrics such as lyocell and recycled polyester. Before you try the trickier fabrics like bouclé, fleece, or polyester satin, use more stable, crisper fabrics to give you confidence, or just dive right in there! You won't enjoy your sewing if you don't love the fabric. If you've set your heart on a delicate fabric and it's not quite right for the project, you can always give it more structure by ironing on interfacing to the wrong side. Lining fabrics should be the same weight or lighter than the main fabric. I have used non-woven medium weight iron-on interfacing and medium loft fusible fleece for the projects in this book. Finally, always try to be inventive with the fabrics you already have and upcycle where you can. Your resourcefulness will inspire more creativity.

## Sewing thread

Good-quality thread is essential, as it will be kind to your machine and run smoothly without any knots or weak spots. Use all-purpose recycled polyester thread. Don't use the little reels you get in a sewing kit or old wooden cotton reels, as poor-quality or old thread can break easily and may harm your machine. When you topstitch (see page 114), do your best to use a thread color that matches the fabric, but for other sewing it's not so important to use a thread color that matches the fabric exactly. It's useful to have neutral colors like cream, beige, or black in your sewing kit.

## Buttons

We all have an eye for a pretty or unusual button so start building a button stash now. You can cut buttons off clothes that are too worn out to pass on or look out for boxes of them in thrift stores.

## Chapter 1

# Home Furnishings and Decorations

Whether you're having a summer party, family celebration, or candlelit dinner, set the perfect scene with your own stylish table linens. You can adjust the dimensions of the runner fabric to tailor-make it to your own table's measurements.

# Napkins and Table Runner

## YOU WILL NEED

**For one napkin:** fabric, 19⅝ x 19⅝in (50 x 50cm) (see steps 1–2 for how to cut an accurate square and see tip for fabric recommendations)

**For the table runner:** fabric, 19⅝ x 98½in (50 x 250cm) (see tip for fabric recommendations)

Matching sewing thread

Basic sewing kit (see page 5)

Set square

Hem gauge

Pointer

Walking foot (optional)

## FINISHED MEASUREMENTS

Napkin: 16⅞ x 16⅞in (43 x 43cm)

Table runner: 16⅞ x 95¾in (43 x 243cm)

## LEARN HOW TO

- Cut out an accurate square
- Press a double hem
- Create a mitered corner
- Topstitch neatly near the edge of the fabric

**1** Draft out a 19⅝ x 19⅝in (50 x 50cm) template, either on graph paper or on plain paper using a set square to get accurate corners. To ensure the square is accurate, fold the paper template into quarters to check that all the sides are equal.

**2** Pin the template to your napkin fabric. If you would like to make several napkins, place all the pieces of fabric together and pin the template on top. Make sure one of the sides of the template is parallel to the selvage (the finished edge of the fabric—see page 112). Cut out the fabric, then remove the pins and template.

*Tips* The fabric for a long runner can be costly if it is in one piece, so you could make it out of two or three pieces of different leftover fabrics. Just remember to add a seam allowance (see page 118) to each piece before you sew them together. Also consider how the fabric designs will join and match together.

Linen has a soft feel and a naturally textured finish for a relaxed look, but you could use any natural fiber such as cotton which is absorbent and washes easily.

Pre-wash your fabric before you cut it. Natural fibers can shrink slightly and you'll want to wash away any finishes on the fabric which may look good but will hinder absorption, especially for the napkins.

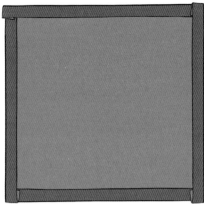

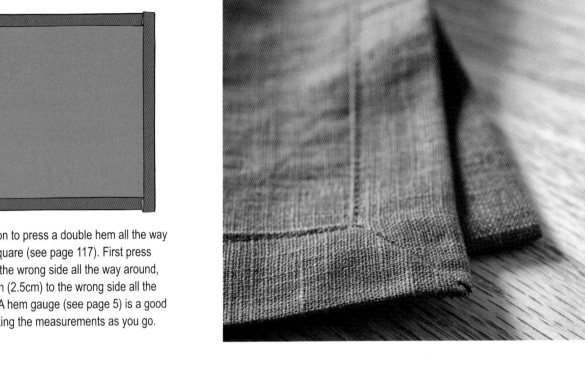

**3** Use an iron to press a double hem all the way around the square (see page 117). First press ⅜in (1cm) to the wrong side all the way around, then press 1in (2.5cm) to the wrong side all the way around. A hem gauge (see page 5) is a good tool for checking the measurements as you go.

**4** Follow steps 1–3 on page 121 to make a mitered corner at each of the four corners on the napkin.

**5** Turn the napkin to the right side and push out all the corners with a pointer. Press all the hems and corners and make sure the seam is pressed flat inside each mitered corner.

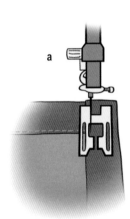

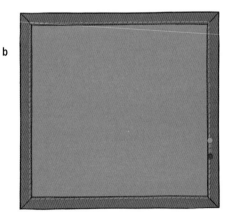

**6** On the wrong side of the napkin, topstitch (see page 114) all around the square very close to the inner folded edges. I used the left-hand side of a walking foot as my guide on the folded edges, with the needle position moved to the left (see a), so I could sew a very short distance away from the folded edge to give a professional finish. You can start topstitching along any side (see b). Pivot with your needle down (see page 116)

when you get to a mitered corner seam, and then continue sewing. You may need to do a few handwheel stitches (see page 115) to get your needle to stop accurately on the corner seam. Overlap your stitches by ⅜in (1cm) when you get back to the beginning. Press your napkin well and repeat with the remaining pieces of napkin fabric, if you are making several.

**7** Once you have cut out the fabric for your table runner, follow steps 3–6 to press the double hem all around the edges, sew the mitered corners, and press the runner well. Using fabric table linen is good for the environment so buon appetito!

Perfect for enjoying a comforting meal or hot drink, these pretty patterned cozies will keep bowls or mugs warm while protecting your hands and the table surface. You can make them in different sizes to fit your favorite bowls or mugs, and they're also easy to stack together and store away.

# Bowl and Mug Cozies

## YOU WILL NEED

**For a small 6in- (15cm-) wide bowl:**
Main fabric, 9⅞ x 9⅞in (25 x 25cm) square
Main fabric, 2½ x 3in (6.5 x 7.5cm) for the tab
Lining fabric, 9⅞ x 9⅞in (25 x 25cm) square
2 pieces of batting (wadding), each 9⅞ x 9⅞in (25 x 25cm) square

**For a large 7in- (18cm-) wide bowl:**
Main fabric, 11¾ x 11¾in (30 x 30cm) square
Main fabric, 2½ x 3in (6.5 x 7.5cm) for the tab
Lining fabric, 11¾ x 11¾in (30 x 30cm) square
2 pieces of batting (wadding), each 11¾ x 11¾in (30 x 30cm) square

**For a 1⅛–3½in- (8–9cm-) wide mug:**
Main fabric, 8¼ x 8¼in (21 x 21cm) square
Main fabric, 2½ x 3in (6.5 x 7.5cm) for the tab
Lining fabric, 8¼ x 8¼in (21 x 21cm) square
2 pieces of batting (wadding), 8¼ x 8¼in (21 x 21cm) square

Matching sewing thread
Basic sewing kit (see page 5)
Walking foot (optional—this makes it easier to sew through all layers but is not essential)
Pressing ham (optional)
Pointer

## FINISHED MEASUREMENTS

Small bowl cozy: 6in (15cm) wide, 2in (5cm) deep
Large bowl cozy: 7in (18cm) wide, 2in (5cm) deep
Mug cozy: 4in (10cm) wide, 2in (5cm) deep

## LEARN HOW TO

■ Mark and quilt fabric
■ Make mini darts
■ Sew through thick layers

**1** Place one piece of batting onto the back of the main fabric square, matching up the edges. Pin or fabric-clip the pieces together. Using a chalk marker and ruler, draw two lines on the right side of the main fabric from corner to corner to make a cross. Topstitch (see page 114) along both of these lines. Remove the fabric clips. Repeat this step with the lining fabric and second piece of batting.

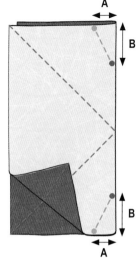

**2** Fold the main square in half. Match up the edges and make sure the main fabric is lying flat inside the batting. Follow the measurements above to mark four dots on the fabric with a pen. Use a ruler and chalk marker to join each pair of dots.

**For the 6in- (15cm-) wide bowl cozy:**
A = 1³⁄₁₆in (3cm)
B = 2in (5cm)
**For the 7in- (18cm-) wide bowl cozy:**
A = 1³⁄₁₆in (3cm)
B = 2⁹⁄₁₆in (6.5cm)
**For the 4in- (10cm-) wide mug cozy:**
A = 1¾in (4.5cm)
B = 1¾in (4.5cm)

Starting at the wider end of each dart, sew along each drawn line, reverse stitching at the start and finish (see page 115).

**3** Now fold the main square in half again, in the opposite direction, so the sewn darts are touching. Mark and sew the same size darts as you did in the previous step along the fold, except on the mug cozy make one of these darts 1in/2.5cm (for A) and 1½in/4cm (for B). This is to allow enough space for the mug handle. Repeat steps 2 and 3 with the lining square.

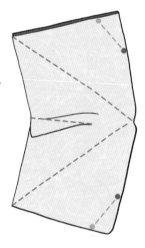

**4** Follow steps 1–3 on page 128 to make a folded strap with the tab fabric. You can really go to town with your fancy machine stitches here if you have them, or just topstitch down each long side of the tab. Here I used a different style of stitch for each the four bowls I made.

*Tips* You can use the same fabric for the tab as for the outside of the cozy, or use a different fabric for the tab.

If you use 100% cotton fabric, batting, and thread, then you can put the cozies in the microwave together with your bowl or mug.

The layers of fabric are quite thick, so fabric clips work better than pins. You can use just one layer of batting for each cozy to make it less bulky for your machine to sew through.

**5** Trim the excess fabric away from the darts on both the main piece and the lining piece. Fold the tab in half and pin it ¾in (2cm) down from one of the main piece's corners, with the loop facing toward the bowl.

**6** Fold the lining bowl inside out, so the dart seams are on the inside of the bowl. Place the lining bowl inside the main-fabric bowl so the right sides of the fabrics are touching.

**7** Use pins to match up the seams of all the darts in the main bowl to the seams of all the darts in the lining bowl (see page 120).

**8** Pin the main and lining fabrics together all the way round the top edge of the bowl, matching the corners together. Using a ⅜in (1cm) seam allowance, sew all the way around the top edge, making sure that you pivot at the corners (see page 116) and go slowly over the darts. Leave a turning gap (of about 2⅜–3⅛in/ 6cm–8cm depending on the size of your cozy) along one side, in between a dart and a corner. Trim the seams, if they are bulky. You may need to layer the seams by trimming the batting shorter than the main and lining fabrics (see page 119). Trim the corners (see page 119).

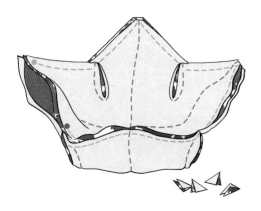

**9** Turn the bowl through to the right side by pulling the fabric out through the turning gap. Use a pointer to point out the corners. This design is quite a difficult shape to press, but press the edges well and use a pressing ham to help you, if you have one (see page 117).

**10** Tuck under the raw edges of the turning gap and pin them together. To finish off your cozy and to close the turning gap, topstitch all the way around the top edge using the right-hand side of your sewing-machine foot as your guide on the edge of the fabric (see page 118). Overlap your stitches when you come round to where you started stitching (see page 115). There are eight pivot points where you will need to change direction, so sew slowly and steadily. To help you sew through all the layers, you can use some handwheel stitches, (see page 115) especially over the darts, or slightly pull the fabric from behind the foot as you sew. You know your machine, so don't push it too hard, and you can always hand-sew the turning gap closed (see page 125). Enjoy your comforting hot drink or warm bowl of food!

# Zippered Pillow

Add a personal touch to your home by sewing your own statement pillow.
You can match it perfectly to your décor, or use contrasting fabrics for
the front and the back to create two different looks.

## YOU WILL NEED

Main fabric for the front, 16⅞ x 24¾in (43 x 63cm)
(choose a heavyweight cotton such as denim, cotton
twill, linen, or velvet)

Contrast main fabric for the back, 16⅞ x 24¾in
(43 x 63cm)

Fusible fleece for the back, 16⅞ x 24¾in (43 x 63cm)

16 x 24in (40 x 60cm) pillow form (cushion pad), or if
you'd like to make your own pillow form, 2 pieces of
fabric (you can use spare/scrap fabric such as an old
bedsheet), each 16⅞ x 24¾in (43 x 63cm)

Approx. 2¼lb (1kg) recycled polyester filling, or reuse
the filling from an old pillow form (give the filling a
good plump up first to loosen the fibers)

Sewing thread in complementary color

20in (50cm) nylon zipper

Basic sewing kit (see page 5)

Quilting guide bar

Zipper foot

Pointer

## FINISHED MEASUREMENTS

15 x 22¾in (38 x 58cm)

## LEARN HOW TO

- Quilt fabric using a quilting guide
- Hand-baste (tack) then sew a zipper in place
- Sew a straight stitch and a zigzag stitch
- Make a pillow form

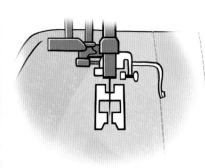

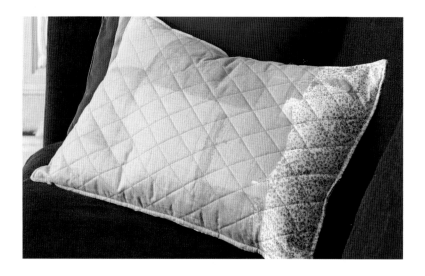

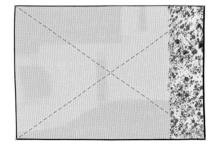

**1** Iron the fusible fleece onto
the wrong side of the fabric for the
back of the pillow. Using a chalk
marker and a ruler, draw two lines
on the right side of the fabric from
corner to corner to make a cross.
Topstitch (see page 114) along
both of these lines.

**2** To start quilting, follow the manufacturer's
instruction to insert the quilting guide bar
into the back of your sewing-machine foot.
I lined up the bar 1½in (4cm) away from
my needle. Place the fabric under the foot
with the guide bar at the start of one of your
diagonal stitch lines. Sew a line, keeping
the guide bar running along the first stitch
line and making sure the bar follows the line
without wobbling. The needle will, in turn,
sew a straight line parallel to the first stitch
line. It's helpful to look at the bar rather than
the needle as you sew. Continue to sew lines
on your fabric, using each row of stitching
as your guide for the next. When you have
finished sewing the lines on one half of the
fabric, rotate the fabric and use the original
stitch line you were following to sew the
lines on the other half of the pillow. Sew
all the lines in one direction first, then
sew the lines in the other direction to
make the grid pattern.

**Tips** In step 4, if you are making a pillow in a different size, make sure you leave at least 2in (5cm) on each side of the zipper (not the zipper tape but where the zipper itself starts and stops).

You can shorten a plastic zipper by sewing over it carefully and reverse stitching.

**3** Decide where you would like your zipper to go—it's usually in the bottom long side of a pillow cover. Sew a line of zigzag stitches (see page 114) on each fabric rectangle separately across the bottom long side, using the right-hand side of your foot as your guide on the edge of the fabric (see page 118). It doesn't matter whether you sew on the right or wrong side of the fabrics.

**4** Place the two fabric rectangles together with the bottom edges aligned. If the quilted fabric has shrunk a little, pin the fabrics together and trim the front piece so that it is the same size as the quilted piece. Draw a line right across the bottom edge, just below your zigzag stitching and ⅝in (1.5cm) away from the raw edge. Find the center of the bottom edge of the fabrics by folding them in half or measuring. Mark the center with a pin. Do the same to mark the center of the zipper. Lay your zipper down onto the quilted side, matching the center marks so the zipper is centered on the fabric. Place two pins at right angles to the bottom edge of the fabrics, to mark where the zipper starts and finishes (not the zipper tape but where the zipper itself starts and finishes).

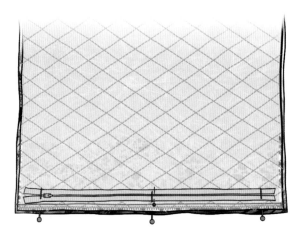

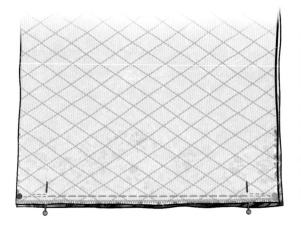

**5** Remove the zipper and the central pins but leave the other pins in place. Sew directly on the drawn line, starting with a normal stitch length (2.4) and reverse stitching at the start (see page 115). When you get to the first pin, sew a few reverse stitches. Then change to a longer "basting" stitch (4) and sew until you get to the second pin. Change back to a normal stitch length (2.4), sew for a few stitches, and then do a few reverse stitches back to the second pin. Then continue sewing until you get to the end and reverse stitch at the finish. The longer stitches make the seam easier to unpick when we reveal the zipper later, and the reverse stitches next to the pins reinforce where the zipper will open and close.

**6** Press the seam open (see page 117). Lay the zipper right-side down on the open seam, with the zipper teeth on the center of the seam. Pin the zipper in place. Hand-baste (tack) (see page 125) all along one side of the zipper, across the teeth, and down the other side through all layers, so that the stitches will show on the right side of the fabrics. Remove the pins.

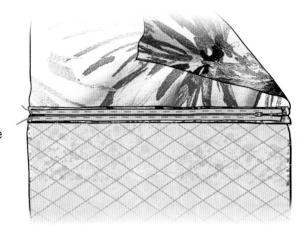

**7** Put the zipper foot on your machine. To sew the zipper in place, we will stitch a long thin rectangle around it on the right side. On the right side of the fabric, use a pin to mark where the zipper pull is. Also use a pin to mark on the right side of the fabric where the other end of the zipper finishes (not the zipper tape but where the zipper teeth finish). This will make sure that you won't sew over any metal staples on the zipper.

**8** Starting on the right side of the fabric at the pin that marks the zipper pull, sew across the zipper. When you start and finish, you may need to accommodate for the bulky zipper pull and sew around it slightly. Pivot (see page 116) and then sew along the first long side about ³⁄₁₆in (0.5cm) away from the seam. When you get to where you've marked the end of the zipper with a pin, pivot, sew carefully across the zipper, and then pivot to sew back along the other long side toward where you started. When you get to the zipper pull end, overlap your stitches where you started (see page 115). When you are sewing down one side and then up the other side, the fabric can pull in different directions. To prevent this, as you sew pull the fabric slightly out at right angles to the zipper.

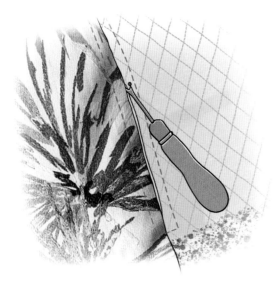

**9** Use a seam ripper to remove all the basting stitches and reveal the zipper. Remove all bits of thread so that they don't get caught in the zipper, and only unpick the seam within the rectangle you have sewn.

**10** Open the zipper and place the back and front fabrics together with the right sides touching, matching the raw edges. Make sure the seams near the zipper lie together and are not folded downward, and pin all the way around. Sew along the sides (except for the side with the zipper), ⅝in (1.5cm) away from the raw edges, using your throat plate as a guide (see page 118). Reverse stitch at the start and finish.

**11** Zigzag stitch all around, in between the straight stitching and the raw edge of the fabric, and trim to the zigzag (see page 119). Do not zigzag stitch along the side with the zipper. If the fabric is bulky, you can trim the corners (see page 119). This will allow you to get your pointer into the corners when you turn the pillow cover right side out, so the finished pillow will have sharp corners. You can also reinforce your straight stitching with another line of straight stitches if necessary.

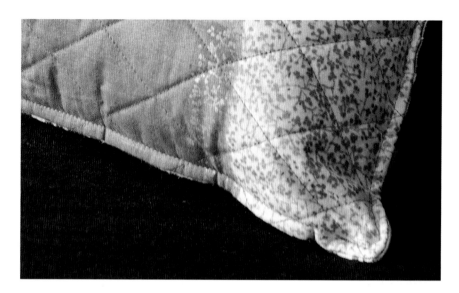

**12** Pull the right side of the fabric out through the open zipper, to turn the pillow cover to the right side. Use a pointer to push out the corners. Give the pillow cover a good press, rolling the seams at the edges so that you can see the stitching and no fabric is left tucked in. To finish off the edges, you can sew "faux piping" by topstitching (see page 114) all the way around the sides without the zipper, using the right-hand side of the sewing-machine foot as a guide on the edge of the pillow cover. Reverse stitch at the start and finish. This gives a more finished look to your cover when the pillow form is inserted.

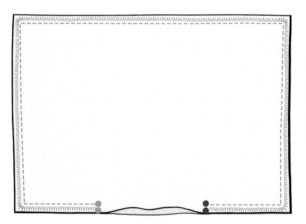

**13** If you are making your own pillow form (cushion pad), place the two pieces of fabric for the pillow form together with the right sides touching. Sew all the way around, using a ⅝in (1.5cm) seam allowance and leaving a 7⅞in (20cm) turning gap along one side (see page 122). Also zigzag stitch around the edge, leaving the same turning gap, to reinforce the seam.

*Tip* Rather than being restricted by standard pillow form sizes, this project shows you how to make a pillow to suit a special nook in your home or the fabulous fabric you want to use. You just need to make a pillow form to go in it (see steps 13–14). If you'd like to make a pillow in a different size, simply change the measurements of the fabric.

**14** Turn the pillow form through to the right side, tuck in the raw edges of the turning gap, and press. Start stuffing the corners with the polyester filling first and then fill in the middle. Pin the turning gap closed and sew about ³⁄₁₆in (0.5cm) away from the edge (see page 122), reverse stitching at the start and finish. If it's difficult to get the pillow form under your machine foot, it may be helpful to put some pins in a short distance away from the first row of pins to keep the filling away from the foot. Insert the pillow form into the pillow cover and close the zipper. Now where's your lovely pillow going to go? Have you earmarked a cozy spot to retreat to?

Skill level ✳

These simple covers are a great way to hide plain planters, revamp your plant pot arrangement, and give your houseplants an attractive new home. They could also be used as storage caddies around the home, in the bedroom or bathroom. One of these would also make a unique gift when combined with a plant.

# Soft Plant Pot Covers

## YOU WILL NEED

**To make a large cover, for a pot/vase that is 7in (18cm) high and 7⅞in (20cm) in diameter:**

Main fabric, 14⅛ x 26¾in (36 x 68cm)

Lining fabric, 14⅛ x 26¾in (36 x 68cm)

**To make a medium cover, for a pot/ vase that is 5½in (14cm) high and 6¼in (16cm) in diameter:**

Main fabric, 10⅝ x 22in (27 x 56cm)

Lining fabric, 10⅝ x 22in (27 x 56cm)

**To make a small cover, for a pot/vase that is 4½in (11.5cm) high and 5⅛in (13cm) in diameter:**

Main fabric, 8⅝ x 16⅞in (22 x 43cm)

Lining fabric, 8⅝ x 16⅞in (22 x 43cm)

Matching sewing thread

Basic sewing kit (see page 5)

Seam roller (optional)

## FINISHED MEASUREMENTS

Large cover: 9½in (24cm) wide, 8in (20cm) deep

Medium cover: 7in (18cm) wide, 5in (13cm) deep

Small cover: 5in (13cm) wide, 4¾in (12cm) deep

## TEMPLATE REQUIRED (SEE PAGE 140)

Corner

## LEARN HOW TO

■ Draft out a rectangle pattern

■ Make a lining

■ Sew a boxed corner

■ Sew a turning gap

**1** Fold the main fabric in half along its length with the right sides of the fabric together, matching up the short sides. Press the piece to make a crease along the fold. You can use an iron or a seam roller for this (see page 117). Repeat with the lining piece.

**2** Pin and then sew down the short sides of the main piece, reverse stitching at the start and finish (see page 115). For the lining piece, place two pins at right angles to the edge of the fabric to mark a 4in (10cm) turning gap in the middle of the short side. Sew along the edge at either side of the turning gap, reverse stitching at each start and finish. Sew along the bottom edge of each piece, reverse stitching at each start and finish.

**3** Put your hand inside the main piece and push out one of the lower corners to create a pointed triangular shape (see step 1 on page 128). Place a pin in the seam, about 2in (5cm) down from the point of the triangle, and push it through to match up with the seam or crease on the other side (see page 120). Smooth out the pointed shape so the two sides are symmetrical. Repeat with the other corner on the main piece. Then repeat this step with the lining piece.

*Tips* If you need to make a bespoke cover for a plant pot or vase that is a different size to the ones above, measure the pot or vase's height and circumference at the widest part. Double the height measurement, and add enough for a seam allowance (see page 118) to the circumference, then cut out a rectangle of fabric with these dimensions. This will give you give you enough fabric for the boxed corners, turnover top, and seam allowances.

Don't use a directional print (see page 113) for the lining fabric, because as you need to turn it over at the top, the design would be upside down.

This project is designed to cover a rigid pot or vase, but if you want it to stand up on its own, iron fusible fleece onto the wrong side of the main fabric to give it more body.

**4** Lay the template on top of one of the triangular points and fix it in place using fabric clips. Draw along the curved edge onto the fabric with a pen. You might find that a cardboard template is easier to draw around. The slightly rounded shape will mean that your cover will sit well around the base of a plant pot. Remove the template from the corner, then repeat this step with the remaining pinned corners on each of the pieces.

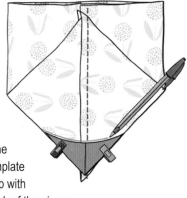

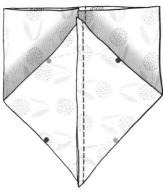

**5**  Sew along each curved pen line on the outer and lining pieces, reverse stitching at each start and finish. Trim away each corner, leaving a ⅜in (1cm) seam allowance.

**6**  Turn the lining piece inside out so the right side of the fabric is on the outside. Insert the lining piece into the main piece, so that the right sides of the fabrics are touching. Match up the two pieces along their top raw edges. Use a pin to match up the pieces along their side seams. Pin all the way around the top edge. Starting at the side seam, sew all the way around the top edge using a ⅜in (1cm) seam allowance and overlapping your stitches (see page 115) by ⅜in (1cm) when you get back to where you started. You might find it easier to use the free-arm attachment on your sewing machine here, if you have one (see page 115). After sewing, trim the seam around the top down to ³⁄₁₆in (0.5cm) (see page 119).

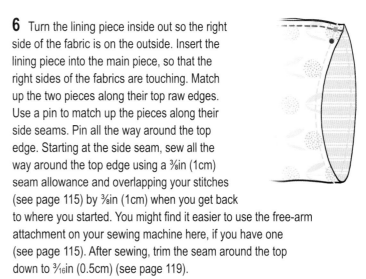

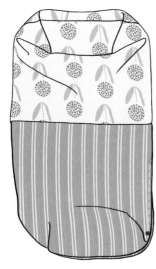

**7**  Pull the right sides of the fabrics out through the turning gap in the lining to turn the plant pot cover to the right side. Tuck in the raw edges of the turning gap (see page 122). Sew the gap closed, using the right-hand side of your sewing-machine foot as your guide on the edge of the fabric (see page 118). Reverse stitch at the start and finish.

**8**  Push the lining inside the main fabric. Press the pot, making sure the main and lining fabrics are level at the top and one is not extending over to the other side more than the other. Fold over the top edge by 1½in or 2in (4cm or 5cm) to suit your plant pot and press the fold in place.

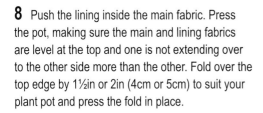

Skill level ✳✳✳

Every pet needs a cozy place to snuggle up and sleep. This project shows you how to make your pet a special spot for snoozing, which they're sure to appreciate. With its ties undone the bed can be laid flat for extra space and comfort in the car or to protect furniture.

# Pet Bed

## YOU WILL NEED

**For the main bed:** fleece fabric (see tip on page 25), 35½ x 44⅞in (90 x 114cm)

**For the straps:** 4 pieces of fleece fabric, each 4 x 11⅞in (10 x 30cm)

**For the pillow:** 2 pieces of fleece or faux fur fabric, each 15¾ x 23⅝in (40 x 60cm)

1lb 2oz–2¼lb (0.5–1kg) recycled polyester stuffing (or reuse the stuffing from an unused pillow form/cushion pad)

Matching sewing thread

Basic sewing kit (see page 5)

Fabric clips

Set square

Ruler

Knitting needle or chopstick

## TEMPLATE REQUIRED (SEE PAGE 136)

Pet Bed diagram

## FINISHED MEASUREMENTS

22½in (57cm) long, 16½in (42cm) wide, 4¾in (12cm) high (with the side bolster pillows upright)

## LEARN HOW TO

- Draft up a pattern
- Sew fleece fabric
- Create a turning gap
- Mark out sewing lines
- Make tube straps
- Stuff the side bolster pillows

**1** Fold the fleece fabric for the main bed in half along its length with the right sides together, so that the 35½in (90cm) folded edge is at the top. Place the template onto the fabric so that the template's long edge is flush with the fold. Pin the template in place. Alternatively, you can draft out the pattern directly onto the fabric as per the diagram on page 136. The template is a 22½ x 35½in (57 x 90cm) rectangle in a landscape orientation with two 6¼ x 6¼in (16 x 16cm) squares cut out from the bottom corners. Cut out the shape from the fabric, keeping the fold intact.

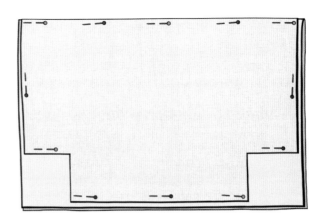

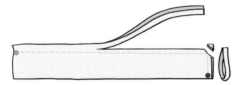

**2** Fold one of the strap pieces in half along its width with the right sides of the fabric together. Sew down the long side, then pivot at the corner (see page 116) and sew along the short side to make a closed tube. Reverse stitch at the start and finish (see page 115). Trim the seam allowance to ³⁄₁₆in (0.5cm) and trim the corner (see page 119). Repeat for the other three strap pieces.

**3** As the tube has a closed end, use the blunt end of a knitting needle or chopstick (blunt end) to push the closed end inside itself. Once you have started pushing it through, it becomes easier and the closed end of the strap will eventually pop out at the other end. Continue pushing the closed end through until the strap is turned out to the right side. Use the knitting needle or chopstick to gently push out the corners, then lightly press the strap on a low heat (see page 117). Fleece fabric can't take much heat so be careful. Repeat with the other straps.

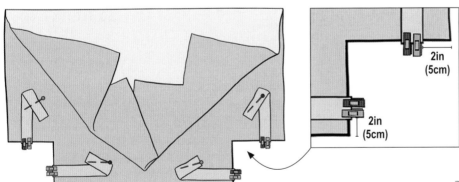

2in (5cm)

2in (5cm)

**4** With your main fabric still folded, lift up the corners of the top layer of fabric to reveal the layer underneath. Position each strap 2in (5cm) in from the outer edges of the fabric. Fix the straps in place with fabric clips, or with pins sticking out at right angles from the outer edges of the fabric. To avoid the straps getting sewn into the seam, pin their free ends in place away from the edges of the main piece.

*Tip*

Fleece fabric is knitted rather than woven, so its stretchy quality can make it tricky to sew. Sew with a small zigzag stitch if your straight stitch is slipping stitches, and don't sew too close to the edge or stretch the fabric as you sew.

**5** Now lower the top layer down on top of the pinned straps to make a fabric "sandwich" with the straps in the middle. Pin all the way around. Place two pins at right angles to the lower edge to mark a 11¾in (30cm) turning gap. Sew along the raw edges, leaving the turning gap unsewn. Reverse stitch at each start and finish (including at either side of the turning gap). Pivot to sew precise corners (see page 116), and go carefully when you sew over the straps.

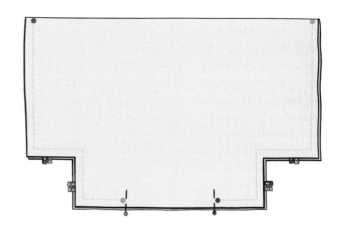

**6** Reinforce the seam at all the corners (see page 119), then trim the outward corners and clip into the inward corners (see page 119). Turn the bed through to the right side by pulling the fabric out through the turning gap, watching out for the pins holding the straps away from the seams. Remove the pins. Point out all the corners and then lightly press the seams on a low heat as before. Tuck in the raw edges of the turning gap by ⅜in (1cm) and lightly press.

**7** To make the side bolster pillows of the bed, using a ruler and a chalk marker (see page 5) or similar that will show up on your fabric, draw a line on each side of the bed from the corner up to the fold at the top. Each line needs to be 5⅞in (15cm) away from the side and parallel to it. On each side along this line, mark 4in (10cm) up from the corner by placing a pin at right angles to the drawn line. Starting at the top edge, sew down the drawn line on each side, stopping at the pin. Reverse stitch at the start and finish. The 4in (10cm) gap on each side will allow you to stuff each pillow, but if you find this gap isn't big enough for you to get your hand in, you can leave a bigger gap.

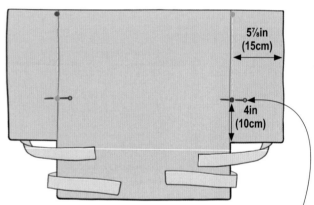

5⅞in (15cm)

4in (10cm)

**Pin at right angles to indicate where to stop, 4in (10cm) before the end**

**8** Pull apart the polyester fiberfill (stuffing) to fluff it up so there are no obvious lumps. Push small amounts of fiberfill through the turning gap in the lower edge and into one of the side sections for the bolsters, through the 4in (10cm) gap at the bottom of the side section. Put small amounts of fiberfill into the corners first then fill in the rest. Try not to stretch the fleece fabric or distort the rectangular shape of the bolster. It's helpful to get your hand in there to help disperse the fiberfill. Repeat to stuff the other side section. When you're happy with the firmness of the stuffing, place pins down each 4in (10cm) gap, on the lines you have drawn. Sew along each line where you've pinned (see tip on page 25), overlapping your existing stitches by ⅜in (1cm) at the start and reverse stitching at the corner.

**9** For the third bolster pillow, use a ruler and a chalk marker or similar to draw a line across the lower section from corner to corner. Sew along this line, reverse stitching at the start and finish. Start stuffing the bolster through the turning gap. Stuff the corners first and then stuff the middle. Use fabric clips to fix together the outer sides of the turning gap so it becomes smaller and you can get more stuffing into the pillow.

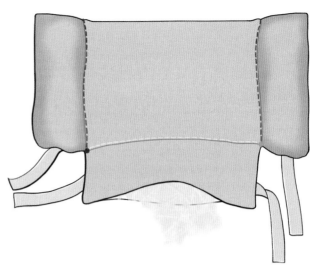

**10** When you're happy with the firmness of the third bolster, use fabric clips to close the remaining part of the turning gap. To close the gap, you can machine-sew along the turning gap (see tip below) or hand-sew it using ladder stitch (see page 125).

**11** Next, you will make the pillow that goes in the middle of the bed. Place the two pieces of fabric for the pillow together with the right sides touching and follow steps 13–14 on page 18 of the Zippered Pillow project. In step 13, leave a 11¾in (30cm) turning gap in the bottom edge of the pillow.

*Tips* You could use fleece throws for the fabric as they are more cost effective, or even better, recycle unwanted ones. Your pet will love you for it!

The bolster pillows in steps 10 and 11 are bulky, so squash each one down to get it under your machine foot and anchor it immediately with your needle and the sewing-machine foot down. Then as you sew, flatten the bolster down to move it along.

You know your pet well, so take into consideration its chewing habits when leaving the bed unattended.

# Garden Kneeler

Easy on the knees and with a handy strap and useful pocket for secateurs, you will always be ready for a spot of gardening with this waterproof kneeler. This project isn't just for gardening—it can be useful for other activities around the home such as picking up toys, home improvements, or sorting the laundry.

## YOU WILL NEED

**For the main sides:** two pieces of waterproof canvas, each 11¾ x 19¾in (30 x 50cm)

**For the pocket:** waterproof canvas, 8⅝ x 11¾in (22 x 30cm)

**For the strap:** 17¾in (45cm) piece of 1¼–2in (3–5cm) wide webbing

Approx. 1lb 2oz (0.5kg) recycled polyester fiberfill (stuffing)

Matching sewing thread

Mug with a diameter of about 3⅛in (8cm)

Basic sewing kit (see page 5)

Ruler

Fabric clips

Hem gauge

Pointer

## FINISHED MEASUREMENTS

11 x 18in (28 x 46cm)

## LEARN HOW TO

- Sew with waterproof fabric
- Topstitch a pocket
- Leave and sew up a turning gap

*Tip* You can use any waterproof fabric such as oilcloth or ripstop fabric, but check that you can sew through it. You may need a walking foot (see page 127) and/or a sharper needle, especially when sewing on the right side such as when topstitching and sewing up the turning gap.

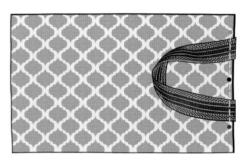

**1** Take one of the pieces for the main sides. Mark the center of one of the short sides by measuring it or folding it in half. Place your webbing strap ends on the raw edge to form a loop, so that each end of the webbing is 2in (5cm) away from the center mark. Fabric clip them in place. Sew along this edge to secure the strap in place, using the right-hand side of the sewing-machine foot as your guide on the edge of the fabric (see page 118).

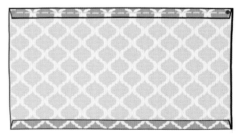

**2** Fold one of the long sides of the pocket piece to the wrong side by ⅜in (1cm). If your fabric can take the heat, press the fold in place using an iron (see page 117). If you're using a fabric that can't be ironed, pin or fabric-clip the folded edge in position. Topstitch (see page 114) along the folded edge on the wrong side of the pocket piece, using the right-hand side of the sewing-machine foot as your guide on the edge of the fabric. Fold the other long side of the pocket to the wrong side by ⅜in (1cm). Press with an iron, finger-press it, or use a seam roller to make the crease stay in place.

**3** Lay the pocket piece on the main piece with the right sides together, so the un-hemmed side is 6¼in (16cm) away from the short side that doesn't have the strap. Fabric-clip or pin the pocket in place along the edges to avoid making any pin holes across the fabric so it remains waterproof. Sew down the crease line on the pocket, reverse stitching at the start and finish (see page 115).

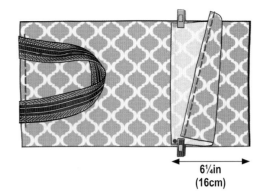

6¼in
(16cm)

**4** Flip the pocket over, along its crease and the row of stitching you have sewn in step 3, so its wrong side is touching the right side of the main piece. Fabric-clip the pocket in place along its short edges. Topstitch close to the edge you have just folded, using the right-hand side of the sewing-machine foot as your guide on the edge of the fold.

**5** On the second main rectangle, mark a ⅜in (1cm) seam allowance all the way around on the wrong side. Use a hem gauge to mark dots at ⅜in (1cm) intervals to help you (see page 118). Then to mark the rounded corners, at each corner use a mug to draw a curve that touches the line at both sides. Place the two main pieces together with the right sides touching. Match up the sides and fabric-clip or pin them together all the way around within the seam allowance. For the turning gap, mark a central dot on the opposite short side to the strap, then mark 3in (7.5cm) on either side from the center to make a 6in (15cm) gap. Starting at the turning gap, sew all the way around on top of the drawn line. Follow your lines exactly to make smooth curves. Reverse stitch at the start and finish.

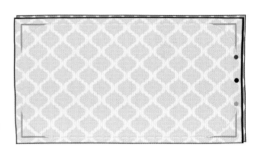

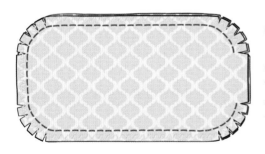

**6** Sew all the way around again with a zigzag stitch (see page 119), in between your row of stitching and the raw edge. Trim the corners to leave a ⅜in (1cm) seam allowance. Clip into the curves, through the zigzag stitching. Turn the kneeler through to the right side by pulling the fabric out through the turning gap. Use a pointer to point out all the curves.

**7** Fill the corners of the kneeler first and then the middle with the polyester fiberfill (stuffing). Fill your kneeler so it is firm, but also make sure the filling has somewhere to go when you kneel on it. If you overstuff the kneeler, the seams may rip! Tuck inside the seam allowance of the turning gap and fabric-clip it in place (see page 122). To close the turning gap, you can either hand-sew it (see page 125) or machine-sew it closed. When using the machine, flatten down the kneeler as much as possible so you can position the sewing-machine foot on the edge. It may be easier to use a zipper foot. Topstitch the turning gap ³⁄₁₆in (0.5cm) away from the edge, reverse stitching at the start and finish.

# Pouffe

This is a chance to use up your fabric scraps and have fun mixing and matching your color palette. The pouffe is the perfect size and height for propping your feet up after a long day at work, or it could be used as additional seating or to rest a tray on. You could make it in fabrics to complement your home décor style, co-ordinating it with matching pillows.

## YOU WILL NEED

**For the top:** 9 pieces of fabric, each 5½ x 5½in (14 x 14cm) (I used one unique square for the middle and then 4 pairs of squares, with each pair in a different fabric)
Iron-on interfacing, 17¾ x 17¾in (45 x 45cm)
Fusible fleece, 17¾ x 17¾in (45 x 45cm)

**For the side strips:** 10 pieces of fabric, each 5½ x 11¾in (14 x 30cm) (I used 3 different fabrics and repeated them in sequence)

**For the side:** Iron-on interfacing, 11 x 49¼in (28 x 125cm)
Fusible fleece, 11 x 49¼in (28 x 125cm)

**For the base:** Circle of suedette fabric, 14⁹⁄₁₆in (37cm) in diameter
Iron-on interfacing, 17¾ x 17¾in (45 x 45cm)
Fusible fleece, 17¾ x 17¾in (45 x 45cm)

Recycled polyester filling, pillow form filling, or chopped-up old rags and scraps of fabric—about 2 kilos are needed but it depends on how firm you want your pouffe to be
Basic sewing kit (see page 5)
Pointer
Ruler

## FINISHED MEASUREMENTS

13in (33cm) tall, 14¼in (36cm) wide

## TEMPLATE REQUIRED (SEE PAGE 139)

Circle

## LEARN HOW TO

- Put together a square patchwork design
- Sew a straight seam onto a circle
- Ladder-stitch the turning gap closed

*Tips* Use suedette fabric for the base of your pouffe for its non-slip qualities.

For a simpler non-patchwork version just use the round template for the top and base. For the sides, measure and cut a rectangle of fabric measuring 11¾in x 49¼in (30 x 125cm).

Make a cardboard template for the squares and/or a rotary cutter to make cutting out more accurate (see page 126).

If you need to cut out the interfacing and/or fusible fleece in more than one piece, ensure they are just butting up and not overlapping when you iron them onto your fabric.

**1** Decide on the arrangement of your nine-patch design. Divide the nine patches into three rows. With the right sides together, sew the three patches of one row together (see steps 3–4 on page 127), and repeat with the other rows.

**2** Put two of the rows together with the right sides of the fabrics touching. Use pins to match up the seams (see page 120) and sew down the whole length, making sure the intersections are as matched up as you can get them. Keeping the pin in until you're a fraction of an inch (a few millimeters) away from the intersection will help you. Repeat to sew on the third row to create the nine-patch design. Press all the seams open (see page 117).

**3** Follow the manufacturer's instructions to iron the interfacing and then the fusible fleece onto the wrong side of your nine-patch square. You can place the interfacing on the wrong side of the nine-patch square, turn it over, and then iron on the right side of the patchwork to melt the glue and fuse the interfacing in place. For the fleece, it works better if you place a cotton cloth (you might have a piece in your stash, or use a piece of sheeting) over the fleece before ironing it onto the interfacing to help it adhere.

**4** Find the center of your patchwork square by placing two rulers from corner to corner and marking the center with a pin. Fold a piece of paper measuring 17¾ x 17¾in (45 x 45cm) into quarters. Lay the quarter circle template onto the folded paper, matching up their corners. Draw around the curve of the template onto the paper, cut it out along the curve through all the layers, and open it out to reveal a full circle with a diameter of 14⁹⁄₁₆in (37cm). Cut out the template. Place the paper circle onto your nine-patch square, matching up the centers. Pin the template in place and cut out the circle from the patchwork piece. Make a pen dot at each quarter mark around the circle edge.

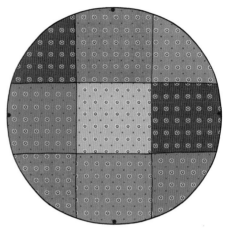

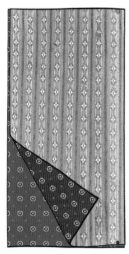

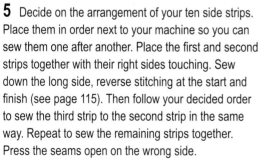

**5** Decide on the arrangement of your ten side strips. Place them in order next to your machine so you can sew them one after another. Place the first and second strips together with their right sides touching. Sew down the long side, reverse stitching at the start and finish (see page 115). Then follow your decided order to sew the third strip to the second strip in the same way. Repeat to sew the remaining strips together. Press the seams open on the wrong side.

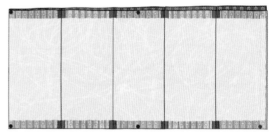

**6** Iron the interfacing and then then the fusible fleece onto the back of the ten-strip side piece (see step 3). They are both narrower than the side strip, so make sure the margin is equal at the top and bottom. Place the short raw edges of the side strip together with the right sides of the fabric touching and pin or fabric-clip in place. Sew down the side with a ⅝in (1.5cm) seam allowance. Reverse stitch at the start and finish and press the seam open. With the piece still folded, mark the top and bottom of the fold along the top and lower edges. Then fold the piece in half (by putting the folded edge onto the side seam) to find and mark the quarter points. If pen or chalk marks don't show up well, mark these points with pins sticking out at right angles to the edges of the fabric.

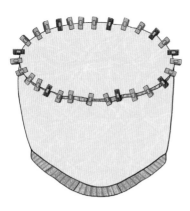

**7** With the right sides together, pin or fabric-clip the patchwork circle top onto the side piece. Match up and then pin or fabric clip the pieces at their quarter marks first and then fill in the gaps. If you are using pins, place them at right angles to the raw edges. You may need to ease (see tip for step 2 on page 58) the side in to fit the top by stretching it a bit as you pin or fabric-clip it in place. Alternatively, you can hand-baste (tack) (see page 125) the layers together instead of pinning or using fabric clips.

**8** Starting anywhere, sew all the way round, overlapping your stitches by ⅜in (1cm) when you get round to the beginning (see step 2 on page 58 of the Bucket Hat project). Sew on the side-strip side, where you might need to slightly stretch or ease in the layers to fit. Go slowly and keep checking that there are no tucks in the fabric on the right side. It is tricky sewing a straight shape onto to a curved shape, but remember that if you have any unwanted tucks at the end, you can unpick them and re-sew that inch (few centimeters) again with a little manipulation. Reinforce your row of stitches (see page 119) by sewing over the top of the first row.

**9** After sewing, clip into the curves (see page 119) and check for any unwanted puckers or tucks. If the fleece has come unstuck at this stage due to all the handling, you can easily press it in place again.

**10** Using the full circle template, cut out the iron-on interfacing and fusible fleece pieces for the base. Fold the interfacing circle into quarters and use a hem gauge to mark dots ⅝in (1.5cm) in from the edge (see page 118). Cut along the dots, through all layers so you have a smaller circle. Repeat with the fusible fleece. Iron the interfacing and then the fusible fleece onto the back of the suedette base circle (see step 3). Ensure the margin is even all the way around. Use the base circle to mark the quarter points with pen dots.

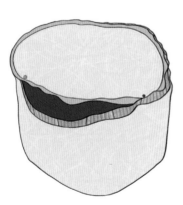

**11** With the right sides together, pin or fabric-clip the base circle onto the open end of the pouffe. Match up the quarter marks first and then fill in the gaps, pinning at right angles to the raw edges. Between one quarter mark and another, leave a turning gap of about 9⅞in (25cm). Start at the turning gap and sew all the way round to the other side of the gap, easing the fabrics to fit each other if necessary. Reverse stitch at the start and finish. Reinforce your stitches by sewing over the top of your existing row.

**12** Clip the curves and check for any unwanted puckers or tucks. Turn the pouffe through to the right side by pulling the fabric out through the turning gap. Push out all the seams with a pointer.

**13** Tease out the stuffing so that it is light and fluffy without any lumps, and push handfuls down and round the edges of the circle. Then gradually fill in the middle up to the top. Get your hand inside to distribute the stuffing evenly and help compact it. Put in as much stuffing as you like (a lot will go in!), deciding how firm you want your pouffe to be.

**14** Tuck the raw edges of the turning gap to the inside and pin or fabric clip in place. With a double-threaded hand-sewing needle (see page 124), use a ladder stitch (see page 125) to sew up the turning gap. Pull up your stitches gently so you don't break the thread. The gap will be under pressure if the pouffe is stuffed firmly, so do a few stitches at a time and pull them up.

Skill level ✻✻

Add a pop of color and style to your dining chairs or patio furniture with this comfortably deep seat pad design with practical tie fastenings.

# Seat Pad

## YOU WILL NEED

### For one seat pad

**For the seat pad:** 2 pieces of soft-furnishing fabric (you can use different fabrics if you wish), each 16⅛ x 16½in (41 x 42cm)

**For the straps:** 4 pieces of fabric, each 2¾ x 9⅞in (7 x 25cm)

Piece of high-density foam with a depth of 2in (5cm), measuring 13¾ x 13¾in (35 x 35cm)

Matching sewing thread

Basic sewing kit (see page 5)

Pointer

Pressing ham

## FINISHED MEASUREMENTS

14½ x 14½in (37 x 37cm)

## TEMPLATE REQUIRED
## (SEE PAGE 134)

Curved Front

## LEARN HOW TO

- Cut foam to size
- Make tube straps
- Sew curved seams
- Create boxed corners
- Use ladder stitch to close a gap

**1** Lay the template on one corner of a piece of the seat pad fabric. Draw round the curve, then cut along the drawn line. Repeat to draw and cut along the second curved corner on the same side of the seat pad fabric. Repeat for the second piece of seat pad fabric.

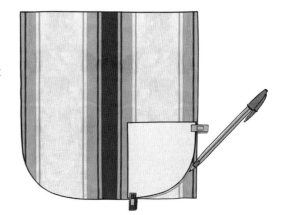

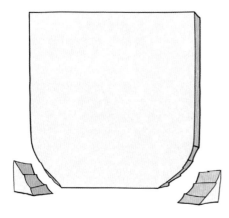

**2** Repeat step 1 to draw and cut two curves on the piece of foam. Cutting through the foam isn't difficult if you use large sharp scissors (and they don't have to be completely smooth curves), but take care when using the scissors. Alternatively, cut out the corner in several goes using a bread knife at right angles to the curve, again taking care.

**3** Fold one short end of a strap piece to its wrong side by ⅜in (1cm) and topstitch in place (see step 1 of the Foldaway Tote Bag project on page 69). Repeat with the other strap pieces.

**4** Follow step 1 on page 128 to fold one of the strap pieces in half along its length with the right sides together. Sew down the long edge and over the fold at the end (see page 129). Reverse stitch at the start and finish (see page 115) and trim the seam to ³⁄₁₆in (5mm). Follow step 2 on page 128 to turn the strap through to the right side using a safety

pin and press. Topstitch down each long side (see page 114) using the right-hand side of the sewing-machine foot on the edge as your guide (see page 118). Don't sew further than the stitched line that is at one end of the strap. Reverse stitch at the start and finish. Repeat with the other strap pieces.

*Tips* To customize your seat pad to fit a different-sized piece of foam, measure the length and height of the piece of foam. Add half of the depth of your foam plus a seam allowance (see page 118) to each of these measurements.

For example:
Foam dimension = Length: 15¾in (40cm) x Width: 15¾in (40cm) x Depth: 1³⁄₁₆in (3cm)

Fabric required:
Length = 15¾in (40cm) + ⅝in (1.5cm) (half of depth) + ⅜in (1cm) (seam allowance) = 16¾in (42.5cm)
Width = the same
Cut out 2 x fabric squares, each measuring 16¾ x 16¾in (42.5 x 42.5cm)

You can omit the curved front of the seat pad and just give it four boxed corners (see step 7) instead.

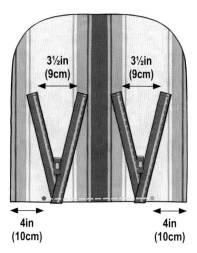

**5** Overlap two of the straps and fabric-clip or pin them together so they make a "V" shape. The ends of the strap should be about 3½in (9cm) apart at the top. Repeat with the other two straps. Along the straight edge and on the right side of one seat pad piece, mark 4in (10cm) in from each side. Position the raw edges of the crossed straps on the raw straight edge of the seat pad at each 4in (10cm) mark. Sew across the straight edge, within the seam allowance, to secure the straps in place.

**6** With the right sides touching, place the two seat pad pieces together, matching up all the raw edges. Tuck the straps inside, making sure they are away from any of the edges. Sew from one strap all the way round to the other strap, pivoting at the two corners (see page 116) and sewing smooth curves. You can use a hem gauge to mark dots along the curves to guide you (see page 118). Reverse stitch at the start and finish. Reinforce your stitches by sewing round the bottom curve again over the first row of stitching (see page 119). Clip into the curves (see page 119).

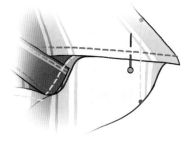

**7** To make the boxed corners, push out one of the corners from the inside with your finger. Secure it by pushing a pin through the seam to match it up with the seam on the other side (see page 120). Draw a line across the corner to make a triangle shape with a 2in (5cm) base line (see page 128). Sew across this base line, reverse stitching at the start and finish. Repeat with the other corner, and then trim the end off each triangle.

**8** Turn the seat pad cover to the right side through the gap, and push out all the corners and curves with a pointer. Press the seams. Use a pressing ham inside the seat pad to press the seams on the outside, especially along the curves.

**9** To get your foam piece inside the cover, roll it up tightly and push the roll inside the seat pad cover, letting it unfold inside. Then maneuver it into position, putting the corners and curves in place first. It may take a few adjustments to get it in position (you will need to get your hand right inside) because the foam does drag on the fabric, but persevere!

**10** Tuck the raw edges of the straps and the raw edges of the turning gap inside (see page 122), and secure the sides of the gap together using pins or fabric clips. Using a ladder stitch (see page 125), hand-sew the gap closed. Sew with the side that hasn't got the straps sewn onto it facing you. As you come to a strap, just continue sewing the ladder stitch. At the end of the gap, do two little stitches in the same place and then dive down into the pad with your needle, pop up farther along the seam, and cut off the thread (see page 124). You could make several of these seat pads for your chairs. Whether you're using them for dinner parties or barbecues, your guests won't ever want to leave!

This jacket will fit snugly around a 8-cup (1 liter) French press, to keep your coffee cozy and warm. It's also designed so you can pour while the jacket is still on. There are two options: a simpler quilted design and a patchwork version. The patchwork version is a great way to use up your fabric stash. You will need 40 small squares, so have fun mixing and matching fabric colors and patterns.

# French Press Jacket

## YOU WILL NEED

### For both versions:

Matching sewing thread

4 pieces of ³⁄₁₆in (0.5cm) wide quilter's tape (double-sided tape), 3½in (9cm) long (optional, to keep the hook-and-loop tape in place while sewing)

Basic sewing kit (see page 5)

Pointer

### For the simple quilted French press jacket:

For the outside: fabric, 9⅞ x 17¾in (25 x 45cm)

For the lining: fabric, 9⅞ x 17¾in (25 x 45cm)

For the hanging loop (optional): fabric, 1½ x 4¾in (4 x 12cm)

Fusible fleece, 9⅞ x 17¾in (25 x 45cm)

3½in (9cm) piece of ¾in (2cm) wide hook-and-loop tape

Quilting guide bar

### For the patchwork French press jacket:

For the outside: 40 squares of fabric, each 2⅜ x 2⅜in (6 x 6cm) (or use ten 4¾ x 4¾in/ 12 x 12cm squares and cut them into quarters. See steps 9–10 for guidance on cutting out the squares.)

For the lining: fabric, 9⅞ x 19¾in (25 x 50cm) (or use eight 4¾ x 4¾in/12 x 12cm squares)

For the hanging loop (optional): fabric, 1½ x 4¾in (4 x 12cm)

Fusible fleece, 9⅞ x 19¾in (25 x 50cm)

3½in (9cm) piece of ¾in (2cm) wide hook-and-loop tape

Quilting ruler

Rotary cutter

Cutting mat

### TEMPLATE REQUIRED (SEE PAGE 138)

French Press Jacket sewing guide

### FINISHED MEASUREMENTS

7 x 14½in (18 x 37cm)

### LEARN HOW TO

- Quilt fabric
- Create a loop
- Use a turning gap
- Topstitch neatly around the edges of the jacket
- Cut out small squares for the patchwork version
- Sew together a detailed patchwork design

## For the simple quilted French press jacket:

**1** Follow steps 1–2 on page 15 of the Zippered Pillow project to iron the fusible fleece onto the wrong side of the outside fabric, then quilt diagonal stitch lines that are ¾in (2cm) apart to create a grid pattern. If you don't have a quilting guide bar, draw the lines for the whole grid pattern using a ruler and chalk marker (see page 127) or mark creases using a hera marker, then sew directly on each line.

> *Tips* Please note that the template is a sewing guide rather than a cutting guide (see page 112).
>
> You could make a smaller version for a two-cup French press (see the template on page 138).

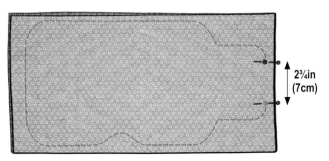

2¾in (7cm)

**2** Place the outside and lining pieces together with the right sides of the fabrics touching, then pin the template on top and draw around it. Remove the template. Put two pins in the flap end, 2¾in (7cm) apart and at right angles to the edge of the fabric to mark a turning gap (see page 122). Sew all the way around on top of your pen line, leaving the turning gap unstitched and reverse stitching at the start and finish (see page 115).

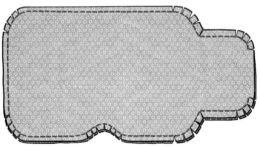

**3** Trim all around the edge of the stitch line, leaving a ⅜in (1cm) seam allowance all around. Snip into all the curves and corners (see page 119), making sure you don't cut through your stitches.

**4** Follow steps 1–2 on page 129 (making a folded strap) to prepare the optional hanging loop.

**5** Turn the jacket to the right side by pulling the fabric out through the turning gap. Push out all the curves with a pointer from the inside. Tuck in the seam allowance of the turning gap, press well (see page 117), and use a pin to fix the turning gap together. If you are adding a hanging loop, use a seam ripper (see page 117) to unpick a ¾in (2cm) gap in the center of the seam on the opposite end to the flap. Fold the hanging loop in half to make a loop. Push the raw ends of the loop into the gap, leaving about 1½in (4cm) of the loop showing. Pin or fabric-clip the loop in place. Topstitch (see page 114) around the edge of the jacket, starting just to one side of the loop and using the right-hand side of the sewing-machine foot as your guide on the edge of the fabric (see page 118). You will close the turning gap as you sew over it. Sew carefully over the hanging loop. Overlap your stitches by ⅜in (1cm) when you get back to the beginning (see page 115).

**6** Now wrap the jacket around your French press to check that it fits. Use a pin to mark where the edge of the flap reaches.

**7** Pins can be difficult to use on hook-and-loop tape, so stick two strips of quilter's tape onto the wrong side of each side of the piece of hook-and-loop tape. This will allow you to stick it in place on the jacket. Position the hook side of the tape on the quilted side of the jacket, in the center of the short straight side, taking note of where your pin is so the jacket fits snugly. The tape should be about ⅜in (1cm) from the short edge.

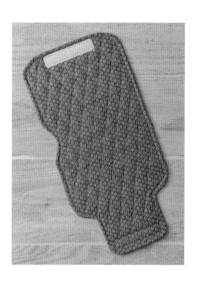

**8** Position the loop part of the tape on the lining side (the non-quilted side) of the flap, close to the edge. Sew all the way around each piece of the hook-and-loop tape as close to the edge as you can. Start on a long side and overlap your stitches by ⅜in (1cm) when you get back to the beginning. Make sure your spool thread color matches the hook-and-loop tape (a light gray isn't as obvious as white) and your bobbin thread color matches the right side of your fabric.

## For the patchwork French press jacket:

**9** Draft out a 4¾ x 4¾in (12 x 12cm) paper template, using graph paper or a set square to give you accurate corners. Cut out the template. Draw around your template onto your fabrics with a pen (see tip on page 37). To help you, you can place a transparent quilting ruler over the top of your template and use a rotary cutter to cut out the squares (see page 126). Alternatively, just mark each of the corners with a dot, use a ruler to join the dots, and then use a quilting ruler and a rotary cutter to cut them out. You could also use the lined grid on your cutting mat to help you cut accurate squares.

**10** Measure and mark the halfway point on each edge of each fabric square, then cut it into four smaller squares. I used a rotary cutter and the lines on my cutting mat to help me for accuracy.

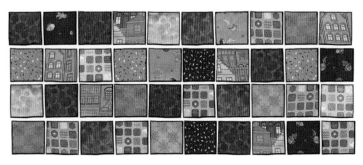

**11** Arrange the squares in four rows of ten squares. Try to avoid placing similar colors together and step back for an objective view, or take a photo of your layout to check that the design is well balanced.

**12** With the right sides of the squares together, start by sewing each row of ten squares together (see page 127). Use the right-hand side of the sewing-machine foot as your guide on the edge of the fabric (see page 118).

**13** When you've sewn the four rows, press the seams in one direction for the first row and then press the next row's seams in the opposite direction and repeat in alternating directions (see page 127). This will prevent any bulky seams when you sew the rows together.

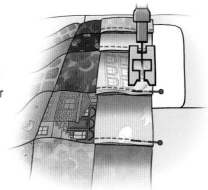

**14** Lay one row onto the next with the right sides together. Use pins to match up the seams (see page 120). Sew down the pinned side, using the right-hand side of your sewing-machine foot as your guide on the edge of the fabric. Sew right up to the pins that are matching your seams together before removing them. Repeat to sew the remaining rows onto the piece.

**15** Press the patchwork piece on the back, keeping the seams facing in the direction they've been pressed and sewn. Then press the front of the patchwork piece. Iron the fusible fleece onto the wrong side of the patchwork piece. Trim the fusible fleece to fit if necessary.

**16** For the lining you can use one piece of fabric measuring 9⅞ x 19⅝in (25 x 50cm), or you can use your 4¾ x 4¾in (12 x 12cm) template to cut eight squares. Follow steps 11–14 to sew them together in two rows of four squares, then press.

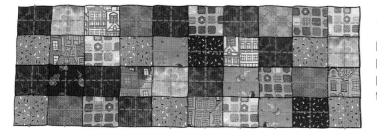

**17** Quilt the outer patchwork piece by topstitching (see page 114) horizontally and vertically down the middle of the patchwork squares. You can use a quilting guide bar (see page 127) to help you position your stitches perfectly down the middle of each square.

**18** Place the outer patchwork piece on top of the lining piece with the right sides together. The two pieces may not be the same size, as the combination of patchwork and quilting often shrinks the dimensions. Choose a good place to lay your French press template down on the fabrics to include all your best patches and matching seams. Draw around the template onto the fusible fleece side, making sure its edges are parallel to the quilting lines. Follow steps 2–8 to sew the patchwork French press jacket. You'll never miss out on a warm fresh coffee again!

*Tip* When placing the square template and cutting out your fabric squares for the patchwork version, make sure you choose the best parts of the fabric designs. As squares get smaller, there is less of the design to see.

## Chapter 2

# Accessories, Bags, and Purses

# Scrunchie

**Make a bold statement with this simple and versatile hair accessory. From satins to velvets, add a flourish to your outfit with your choice of fabric for this project.**

## YOU WILL NEED

Fabric, 5⅛in x 23⅝in (13 x 60cm)

6¼in (16cm) piece of ¼–⅜in- (0.7cm–1cm-) wide elastic

Matching sewing thread

Basic sewing kit (see page 5)

2 safety pins

## FINISHED MEASUREMENTS

1½in (4cm) wide, 13in (33cm) outer circumference

## LEARN HOW TO

- Turn through a tube
- Thread elastic with a safety pin
- Sew a seam with reverse stitch
- Sew up an opening

3⅛in (8cm)        3⅛in (8cm)

**1** Fold the rectangle of fabric in half along its width with the right sides of the fabric touching. Measure 3⅛in (8cm) in from each short side. Place a pin in the fabric at right angles to the top edge at each of these points. Pin and then sew in between the two pins using a ⅜in (1cm) seam allowance, leaving 3⅛in (8cm) unsewn at each end. Reverse stitch at the start and finish (see page 115).

**2** Use a safety pin to turn the fabric tube through to the right side (see page 128). Open out the short ends and place them together with their right sides touching. Pin and sew down the edge using a ⅜in (1cm) seam allowance, reverse stitching at the start and finish.

**3** Press the seam open (see page 117). Tuck the seam allowances along the opening to the wrong side of the scrunchie.

**4** Pin together one side of the opening up to the seam, leaving the other 3⅛in (8cm)-long half of the opening unpinned and still open. Using the right-hand side of your sewing-machine foot as your guide on the edge of the fabric (see page 118), topstitch (see page 114) along the pinned edge to close half of the opening. Reverse stitch at the start and finish. Pin a safety pin onto each end of the piece of elastic. Also pin one of the safety pins to the scrunchie fabric, so you don't lose the end of the elastic. Feed the other safety pin inside the scrunchie and push it round the fabric tube, making sure the elastic doesn't get twisted inside.

**5** When the elastic has popped out of the other end of the gap, remove both safety pins. Making sure that you do not let go of the elastic ends, tie them together in a double knot so they are secure. If your elastic is thicker than ¼in (7mm), it is better to sew the ends of the elastic together. Pull out the elastic as far as you can, then pin the ends together. Zigzag stitch across the ends and then reverse stitch over your first stitch line.

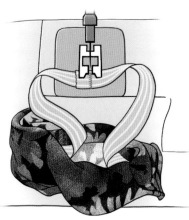

**6** Pull the scrunchie so the elastic goes inside it. Tuck the raw edges of the opening to the inside of the scrunchie by ⅜in (1cm) and pin them together. Using the right-hand side of the sewing-machine foot on the edge of the fabric, sew the edges together to close the gap. Reverse stitch at the start and finish. Windy day? Grab that scrunchie! Your hair is not going to be a problem!

*Tips* If you haven't got a 23⅝in (60cm) long piece of fabric, you can cut the fabric for the scrunchie out in two pieces, but remember to add a ⅜in (1cm) seam allowance (see page 118) to both short sides before you stitch them together.

Make different sized scrunchies for different occasions—just experiment with the length and width of the piece of fabric and consider how many times you want to twist the scrunchie around your hair.

Skill level ✳ *Stashbuster*

This handy wristlet is the perfect way to keep your keys within easy reach. You could make several and attach them to anything to make carrying easier, such as a coin purse or a water bottle. One of these wristlets would also make a stylish addition to your handbag.

# Key Fob Wristlet

## YOU WILL NEED

Main fabric, 2 x 14in (5 x 36cm)

Lining fabric, 2 x 14in (5 x 36cm) (you can use the same fabric for the main and lining pieces, as I have done in these steps, or use a contrast fabric for the lining)

Sewing thread in complementary color

1¼in (3cm) wide swivel clip

Basic sewing kit (see page 5)

Pressing ham (optional)

Pointer

## FINISHED MEASUREMENTS

1¼in x 6½in (3 x 16.5cm)

## TEMPLATE REQUIRED (SEE PAGE 132)

Strap

## CUTTING GUIDE

Cut 1 x Strap on fold in each of the main fabric and lining fabric

## LEARN HOW TO

■ Sew a tube and turn it through to the right side

■ Press a tube

■ Topstitch

■ Sew through thick layers

*Tip* Lightweight fabrics will be easier to work with for this project because there are some thick layers to sew through.

**1** Place the main fabric and lining strap pieces together with their right sides touching.

**2** Before you start sewing, mark one end of the strap with a pen dot in the center, and then mark two dots at ½in (1.25cm) on either side of the central mark. Repeat to make the same marks on the other end of the strap. The ends are tapered to be 1in (2.5cm) wide so they will easily fit through the swivel clip. Sew along each side of the strap, using the right-hand side of your sewing-machine foot as your guide on the edge of the fabric (see page 118). Sew a gentle curve at each end, so that you start and finish at the outer dots on the end of the strap. Trim the corners (see page 119).

**3** Press the wristlet piece to set your stitches (see page 117) and then use a safety pin to turn the tube to the right side (see page 128). If you've chosen a stiff fabric, this may be tricky, but go slowly and release the bunched-up gathers every so often.

**4** Use a pointer to push out the ends so you can see they are tapered. Press the strap so that the fabric doesn't peep round more on one side (this is especially important if you are using two different fabrics). Topstitch (see page 114) down each long side as near as you can to the edge, or use the right-hand side of the sewing-machine foot as your guide on the edge of the fabric.

**5** Thread a swivel clip onto the strap. With the main-fabric sides touching (if you are using different fabrics for the outside and lining), fold the strap in half, place the two short ends of the strap together, and pin in place. Using a ⅜in (1cm) seam allowance, sew along the short end carefully as the layers may be thick. Use some handwheel stitches (see page 115) if necessary to get over the bulkiness. Reverse stitch at the start and finish (see page 115).

**6** Open out the two raw edges of the seam, and press the seam open (see page 117). You may find a pressing ham useful here to help you press. Position the D-shaped ring of the swivel clip in between the two raw edges of the seam.

**7** Fold the strap around the D-shaped ring of the swivel clip, with the seam on the inside of the strap. Pin or fabric-clip the two sides of the strap together. Butt up the sewing-machine foot against the D-ring so you can get as close to it as possible. Topstitch a straight line across the strap, close to the D-ring, reverse stitching at the start and finish. If the fabric layers are too thick to reverse-stitch through, you can just tie the loose ends of the threads together in a double knot and trim them. Alternatively, you can sew across the strap, then leave your needle down and lift up the presser foot. Then turn the strap around, put the presser foot down, and sew back over your stitches in the opposite direction.

This little personalized notebook is perfect for jotting down memos. Whether you're using your notebook for ideas, lists, or doodles, you can choose fabrics to suggest what it's for, or just make it stand out so you don't lose it! As it's reversible, you could think of two themes for your cover.

# Reversible Notebook Cover

## YOU WILL NEED

### For a 4⅛ x 6in/UK A6 notebook:

Two pieces of contrasting fabric, each 7½ x 14⅛in (19 x 36cm)

Fusible fleece, 7½ x 14⅛in (19 x 36cm)

Sewing thread in complementary color

Basic sewing kit (see page 5)

4⅛ x 6in (UK A6) hardback notebook

Pointer

## FINISHED MEASUREMENTS

6¼ x 9¾in (16 x 25cm)

## LEARN HOW TO

- Leave a turning gap
- Sew thick fabrics
- Sew up a turning gap

**1** Iron the fusible fleece onto the wrong side of the fabric rectangle you would like to quilt.

**2** If desired, stitch quilting lines on the fabric you have ironed the fusible fleece onto. You can choose to quilt a grid pattern (see page 127). Alternatively, if you have chosen a fabric with stripes, you can follow the lines of the stripes to sew your quilting lines (as I have done in this project).

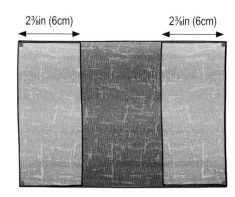

**3** On the wrong side of the non-quilted rectangle of fabric, mark dots 2⅜in (6cm) in from each short side on the top and lower edges. Fold each side at the pen dots with the right sides of the fabric touching. Press the two folds (see page 117). Repeat with the quilted fabric rectangle. When ironing the fusible fleece side, place a piece of cotton cloth (you might have a piece in your stash, or use a piece of sheeting) on top before you iron.

*Tip* This cover fits a hardback 4⅛ x 6in (UK A6) notebook. If you'd like to make a cover for a notebook that's a different size, follow these instructions to find out the length and width of the fabric you'll need:

FABRIC LENGTH: With the notebook closed, measure all the way around, from the edge of the front cover to the edge of the back cover. Add 1¼in (3cm) (for both of the seam allowances) plus 2 x 2–2¾in (5–7cm) (for the inside flaps).

FABRIC WIDTH: Measure the height of your notebook and add 1⅝in (4cm).

Draw out a rectangle with these measurements on your fabrics and fusible fleece, then cut them out. Follow the steps to make your notebook cover, sewing with ⅝in (1.5cm) seam allowances (see page 118).

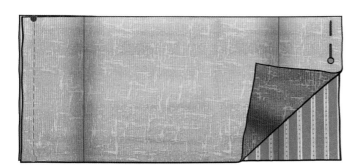

**4** Flatten out the rectangles and place them together with their right sides touching. Pin and then sew down one of the short sides, using a ⅝in (1.5cm) seam allowance and reverse stitching at the start and finish (see page 115). Repeat to sew along the other short side.

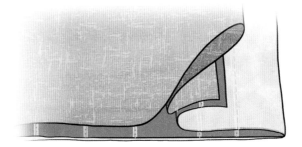

**5** Push one of the side seams in between the two layers so that the creases will line up. Make sure the seam is folded exactly along its center, to avoid one fabric peeping round more on one side. Repeat on the other side.

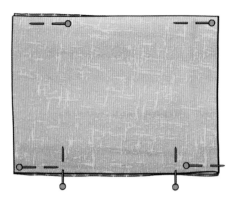

**6** Flatten the cover so that the folds match up along the sides. Pin in place across the top and bottom of the cover. Measure 2¾in (7cm) in from each side on one of the long edges (at the bottom if your fabric has a directional print) and mark these points with a pin at right angles to the edge of the fabric.

**7** At this point wrap the cover around your notebook to check that it fits well. You can make adjustments if necessary by sewing the side seams with a larger seam allowance to make it smaller or by not tucking the sides in so much to make it bigger. Notebooks and the depth of their spines differ, so you may need to tweak the size. It's important that the cover is roomy because you want the book to be able to close fully.

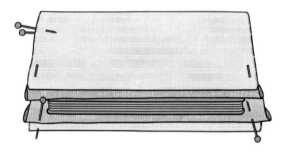

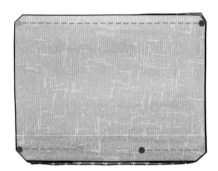

**8** Remove the notebook and open out the cover again. Using a ⅝in (1.5cm) seam allowance, sew where you've pinned across the top and bottom, reverse stitching at each start and finish. Remember to leave the turning gap unsewn. Trim the seam allowance down to ⅜in (1cm) and cut off the corners (see page 119).

**9** Turn the cover to the right side by pulling the fabric out through the turning gap. Use a pointer or similar to point out all the corners. Press the cover on both sides, making sure one fabric doesn't peep around more to the other side. Tuck in the raw edges of the turning gap neatly and pin in place (see page 122). Topstitch (see page 114) the turning gap closed as near to the edge as you can, to give it a neater finish. Reverse stitch at the start and finish.

A comfy pair of slippers is always an essential for a weekend away or a vacation. These cozy slippers are flexible, easy to pack, and the suedette fabric used for the sole makes them anti-slip.

Skill level ✹✹✹

# Cozy Slippers

## YOU WILL NEED

Main fabric, 19¾ x 24½in (50 x 62cm) (I used cotton velvet)

Lining fabric, 19¾ x 24½in (50 x 62cm) (I used cotton)

Fabric for the outer sole (use suedette, which is a super-soft faux suede, or similar non-slip durable fabric), 11¾ x 11¾in (30 x 30cm)

Fusible fleece, 19¾ x 24½in (50 x 62cm)

Matching sewing thread

Basic sewing kit (see page 5)

Walking foot (optional)

## TEMPLATES REQUIRED (SEE PAGE 140)

Top

Sole

## CUTTING GUIDE

Cut 2 on fold in each of the main fabric, lining fabric, and fusible fleece:

Top

Cut 2 in each of the lining fabric, fusible fleece, and outer sole fabric:

Sole

## NOTE

These slippers fit a women's US size 7.5–8.5/UK size 5–6/ EU size 38–39.5

To make the slippers in a different size, you can draw around your own foot and use that as your guide. To keep the slipper proportions accurate, copy the slipper top and sole templates onto one sheet of paper. Enlarge or reduce the templates so that the sole piece fits the outline of your foot, with enough space for a seam allowance all the way around (see page 118).

## FINISHED MEASUREMENTS

Length of sole: 9in (23cm), width at widest point: 3½in (9cm)

## LEARN HOW TO

- Create mini darts
- Sew through fabric layers
- Sew the curve of the heel
- Close the turning gap with a whipstitch

**1** Iron the two fusible fleece slipper top pieces onto the wrong sides of the main-fabric slipper top pieces (see step 3 on page 29). Iron the two fusible fleece sole pieces onto the wrong sides of the two lining sole pieces.

**2** Use pen dots to transfer the template markings, except for the turning-gap markings on the sole and the dart markings on the top, to the right side of all the pieces (see page 113). Transfer the turning-gap markings to the wrong side of the two outer sole pieces only.

**3** Fold one of the main-fabric top pieces in half with the right sides together, making sure there are no wrinkles inside the fold. Use a pen to transfer the dart markings on the template to the folded edge. Use a

ruler to join the dots. Starting from the widest part of the dart, sew down the drawn line, reverse stitching at the start and finish (see page 115). Repeat with the other main-fabric slipper top and with the two lining slipper tops.

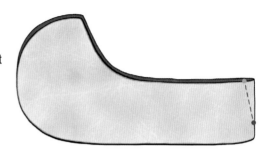

**4** Trim the excess fabric away from each of the darts on the slipper top pieces.

**5** Place together one main-fabric top piece and one lining top piece with the right sides touching. Make sure the dart seams are open and that the pieces match up along the edges. Pin and then sew along the inner curved edge. To help you sew a smooth curve, you can use a hem gauge to mark dots around the curve, ⅜in (1cm) away from the edge, then sew through the dots (see page 118). Repeat with the other main-fabric and lining top pieces.

**6** Clip into the curves (see page 119) and then flip one of the slipper top pieces over along the stitch line, so the wrong sides of the fabrics are touching. Press the seam, using your fingers to roll out the seam so it's not tucked in (see page 117). Pin or fabric-clip the raw edges together, making sure all the layers match up. To keep the layers together, sew close to the raw edge using the right-hand side of your sewing-machine foot as your guide on the edge of the fabric (see page 118). Repeat with the second slipper top piece.

**7** Place the lining sole pieces on the table with the right sides facing upward. Lay a slipper top, with the right side facing upward, on top of each sole piece. Overlap the front edge of one slipper top one way, and overlap the front edge of the other slipper top the opposite way, so the slippers are a mirror image of each other. Match up the central markings at the top of each slipper. Also match up the marking at the bottom of each sole with the dart seam at the heel of each slipper top.

Fabric-clip or pin the layers together. Sew all the way around each slipper, using the right-hand side of the sewing-machine foot as your guide on the edge of the fabric. Start at the side where the layers aren't so thick, and overlap your stitches by ⅜in (1cm) when you get back to where you started (see page 115). Sew carefully around the heel—you may need to stop a few times with the needle down to move the fabric out of the way so that you can continue sewing.

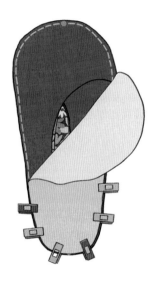

**8** Place one suedette outer sole piece over one of the slippers with the right sides touching. Pin or fabric-clip it in place all the way around, matching up the central notches at the toe and heel. You will need to squash the slipper top down flat to allow you to fit the sole over it. Repeat with the second suedette outer sole piece and the second slipper.

**9** Using a ⅜in (1cm) seam allowance, sew all the way around on the outer sole side, leaving a 4in (10cm) turning gap along one side (as per the template markings) and reverse stitching at the start and finish. You may want to use a walking foot on your sewing machine if you have thick layers of fabric (see page 127). When it is squashed down, the slipper top will have a few folds in the fabric at the heel, so sew a bit closer to the edge at the heel to avoid any unwanted tucks. Repeat with the other slipper, leaving the turning gap in the opposite side.

**10** Turn one slipper through to the right side by carefully pulling the fabric out through the turning gap. It may be tricky to pull everything through, so take your time and try not to break any stitches. Check that all the layers have been caught into the seam, especially on the slipper top where you will see the seam. Repeat to turn the other slipper through to the right side.

**11** To close the turning gap on each slipper, tuck in the raw edges and pin them in place. Hand-sew the gap closed using whipstitch with the smallest and neatest stitches you can do (see page 125). Now where's that slumber party? Who's up for a mini-break? Which way to the spa?

*Tips* Sewing through the thick layers may be difficult, so for your first pair of slippers, choose a medium-weight fabric such as quilting cotton and swap the fusible fleece for iron-on interfacing.

Using a walking foot on your sewing machine will help you sew through the fabric layers.

# Sleep Mask

**A good sleep mask should block out the light and feel comfortable over your eyes. Create your own bespoke mask so that you can get some hard-earned shut eye!**

## YOU WILL NEED

Main fabric for the mask, 6 x 9⅞in (15 x 25cm)

Main fabric for the elastic casing, 2 x 19⅝in (5 x 50cm)

Main fabric for the frill, 2⅜ x 33½in (6 x 85cm)

Lining fabric, 6 x 9⅞in (15 x 25cm)

Fusible fleece, 6 x 9⅞in (15 x 25cm)

13¾in (35cm) piece of ⅜in (1cm)-wide elastic (or measure your head to find the exact length you will need—see step 9)

Basic sewing kit (see page 5)

Fabric clips

Pointer

## FINISHED MEASUREMENTS

4⅜ x 8¼in (11 x 21cm)

## TEMPLATE REQUIRED (SEE PAGE 134)

Mask

## CUTTING GUIDE

Cut 1 x Mask in each of the main fabric, lining, and fusible fleece

## LEARN HOW TO

- Sew curves
- Make a frill with a gathering stitch
- Create a turning gap
- Make an elastic casing

*Tips*  Choose a lining fabric that will be soft on your skin. Silk is perfect (you could use an old silk scarf), but cheaper alternatives such as polyester satin or cotton lawn will be just as soothing.

This project involves making a frill on a small scale, but the technique can easily cross over to larger items such as garments. For example, you could add a frill to a dress hem or down the side of a button band—try it!

Leave out the frill if you want to make a simpler mask. Just follow step 1, then continue with the instructions for steps 6–14.

**1** Iron the fusible fleece onto the wrong side of the main-fabric mask piece.

*Tip* The important things to remember with the two parallel lines of stitching in step 2 is that they should start and stop ⅜in (1cm) away from each short edge, they should be parallel and not cross over each other, and you should not reverse stitch at either end.

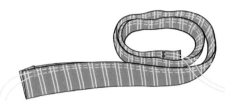

**2** Fold each short end of the frill fabric to the wrong side by ⅜in (1cm) and press (see page 117). Then fold the frill fabric in half along its width with the wrong sides touching and press. To make gathering stitches, choose a long stitch (4+) on your machine's stitch-length dial and a looser tension (2 or 3) on your tension dial. Sew along the long raw edge using the right-hand side of your sewing-machine foot as a guide on the edge of the fabric (see page 118). Start sewing ⅜in (1cm) in from the short edge and stop ⅜in (1cm) before you reach the other short edge. Sew a second row of the same long stitch ⅛in (a few millimeters) away from your first stitch line, keeping within the seam allowance. Do not snip away the loose threads at either end.

**3** On one side of the frill, take two of the threads from one side of one end of your stitched lines and start pulling them up to form a gather. If the two row of stitches don't stop at the same place, unpick a few stitches so they are level. Do the same with the two threads at the other end. This way you are pulling up the stitches from both sides so the gathers can meet in the middle. Take turns pulling each pair of threads up to form a gather, pulling the two threads at each side evenly as one. If the stitches are tight or the fabric is stiff or thick, it will be more difficult to make gathers and the threads are more likely to break, so go slowly. The frill needs to be about 18⅞in (48cm) to fit around the mask, so keep checking its length as you draw up the stitches.

**4** When the frill measures 18⅞in (48cm), take the two threads you've been pulling at one end and tie them in a double knot. Do the same with the two threads at the other end. Cut off the long threads. Because you've now fastened the ends, you can move the gathers along with your fingers to evenly distribute them along the frill. Check that the gathers are even all the way along and that there isn't a big bunch of them in one place or a flat area in another.

**5** Place the main-fabric mask piece on the table with the right side facing upward. Place one end of the frill on the lower side of the mask, left of center. Match up the raw edges and pin or fix in place using a fabric clip. Continue to pin or fabric-clip the frill in place all the way around the mask piece, then overlap the two ends of the frill by ⅜in (1cm) and pin or fabric-clip them in place. If you need to trim the frill to fit, make sure you leave enough fabric so that you can fold the end of the frill to the wrong side by ⅜in (1cm) (to hide the raw edge) and that the two ends will overlap by ⅜in (1cm) so there isn't a gap. Once pinned or fabric-clipped in place, starting anywhere, sew clockwise all the way around on the frill side using a ⅜in (1cm) seam allowance. Overlap your stitching by ⅜in (1cm) when you come round to where you started (see page 115).

*Tips* As you sew around the mask in step 5, make sure the gathers stay even and aren't more bunched up in one area. If they are, you can move the gathers along with your fingers to evenly distribute them.

Also check that the gathers are at right angles to the raw edge, they don't slope to one side, and that there are no big tucks in the frill. If you can see any irregularities, stop with your needle down and redistribute the gathers.

Remove your pins or fabric clips in time so that they don't affect your sewing line (see page 113).

**6** Fold the fabric for the casing in half along its width with the right sides together. Pin and then sew down the long raw edge, using a ⅜in (1cm) seam allowance (see step 1 on page 128 for making a tube strap). Turn the casing through to the right side using a safety pin (see step 2 on page 128 for making a tube strap).

**7** Wrap the piece of elastic around the back of your head to the front of your ears, where the mask will sit. Stretch it a little to make sure it's comfortable and trim the elastic if necessary. Pin a safety pin onto each end of the elastic. Thread one end into the casing and feed it through to the other end. The second pin will ensure you don't lose the other end inside the casing. Make sure the elastic isn't twisted inside and, when it's level with the end of the casing, remove the safety pin and fix the elastic in place at the end of the casing with a pin. Sew across the end of the casing ⅜in (1cm) from the end and then reverse back over your stitching to secure the elastic.

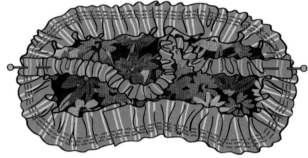

**8** Pull the other end of the casing fabric to let the remaining exposed length of elastic disappear into the casing, so that the end of the elastic is level with the raw edge of the fabric. Make sure the elastic isn't twisted inside the casing, then remove the second safety pin. Pin the end of the elastic to the end of the casing and sew across it, as you did for the first end. Even out the wrinkles along the casing fabric.

**9** Using the template, mark the side notches on the frill with pen dots (see page 113). At the marked dots, pin the ends of the elastic casing at right angles to the frill. Make sure that the elastic casing is not twisted.

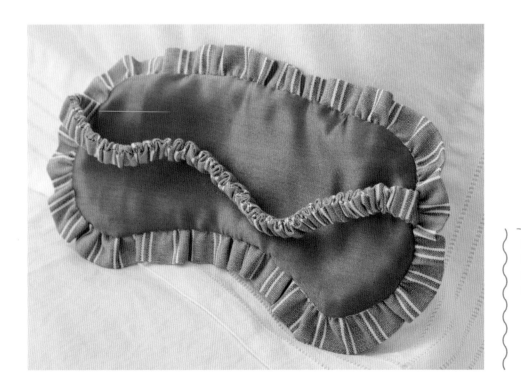

*Tip* Make sure you follow the curves of the shape of the mask as you sew around it in step 11, especially at the lower edge.

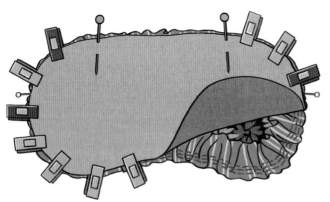

**10** Place the lining fabric right side down onto the mask. Fabric-clip or pin the lining in place (at right angles to the edge of the mask), matching up all the raw edges. Mark a 4in (10cm) turning gap (see page 122) in the top straight edge with two pins at right angles to the top edge.

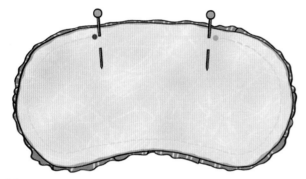

**11** Turn the mask over. On the fleece side, sew all the way around on top of your existing stitch line, keeping the curves smooth. Start at one side of the turning gap and reverse stitch at the start and finish (see page 115), leaving the turning gap unsewn.

**12** Trim the seam all around the edge and clip into the curves (see page 119). The layers are thick, so just snip through a few layers at a time to avoid accidentally cutting through your stitches.

**13** Turn the mask to the right side by pulling the fabric out through the turning gap. Push out all the curves with a pointer. Tuck the raw edges of the lining at the turning gap in by ⅜in (1cm) and pin or fabric-clip them in place (see page 122).

**14** With a hand-sewing needle and single thread, hand-sew the gap closed with small whipstitches about ⅜in (1cm) apart (see page 125). Make sure you pick up a tiny amount of the frill fabric for each stitch and that the stitches don't show on the right side of the mask. Fasten off by making two stitches in the same place, then push the needle down, bring it up a short distance along the seam, and cut the thread (see page 124). After all that hard work you now have the most elegant way to block out light for a perfect night's sleep.

A classic neck tie puts the perfect finishing touch to an outfit. Choose a distinctive fabric to make a sharp impression or one with an informal design to lift the mood! There are two tie shapes to choose from—a regular neck tie and a skinny version.

### YOU WILL NEED

**For the skinny neck tie:**

For the outside: fabric, 23¾ x 23¾in (60 x 60cm) (see tips on page 56)

For the lining: fabric, 6 x 9⅞in (15 x 25cm)

For the keeper loop: fabric, 4⅜ x 2in (11 x 5cm)

**For the regular neck tie:**

For the outside: fabric, 25⅝ x 29½in (65 x 75cm) (see tips on page 56)

For the lining: fabric, 10 x 13¾in (25 x 35cm)

For the keeper loop: fabric, 5½ x 2in (14 x 5cm)

Matching sewing thread

Basic sewing kit (see page 5)

### FINISHED MEASUREMENTS

Skinny Tie: 56in (142cm) long, 2in (5cm) at widest point

Regular Tie: 61in (155cm) long, 4⅜in (11cm) at widest point

### TEMPLATES REQUIRED (SEE PAGE 133)

Skinny Tie Front (includes Front Lining template)

Skinny Tie Middle

Skinny Tie Back (includes Back Lining template)

Regular Tie Front (includes Front Lining template)

Regular Tie Middle

Regular Tie Back (includes Back Lining template)

### CUTTING GUIDE

Cut 1 of each of the following in the main fabric: Front, Middle, and Back

Cut 1 of each of the following in the lining fabric: Back Lining and Front Lining

Please note this project is suitable for non-directional prints (see page 113).

### LEARN HOW TO

■ Lay out a pattern on the bias

■ Handle and sew fabric cut on the bias

■ Make a keeper loop

■ Turn a fabric tube to the right side

**1** Each neck tie is made up of three pattern pieces which are sewn together, and two lining pieces for the tie ends. All the pattern pieces are cut on the bias which means they are placed diagonally across the fabric at 45 degrees from the selvage edge (see page 112) of the fabric. Cutting out the tie on the bias allows it to stretch a little around the neck, helping it lay flat and stay comfortable when worn. The grainline (shown by a double-ended arrow) on the templates indicates how the pattern pieces should be placed on the fabric. Lay out and pin your templates to the fabric, making sure the grainlines run parallel to the selvage. Cut out the pieces from the fabric. You can cut out the two lining pieces in a contrast fabric or keep them the same as the main fabric.

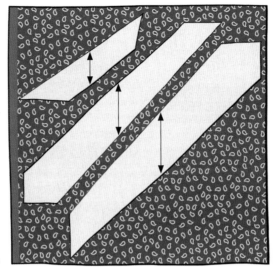
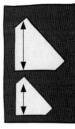

**2** If you are using a very lightweight fabric, pin the three non-lining template pieces to a piece of lightweight fusible interfacing and cut them out. Non-woven interfacing does not have a grain so it doesn't matter which way you place the pattern pieces. Iron the fusible interfacing pieces onto the wrong sides of the three main pieces.

**3** Transfer all the single and double notch markings to the fabric pieces with pen dots (see page 113). Pin or fabric-clip the three main pieces of the tie together, using the single and double notches to align them. Sew down the two seams using a ⅜in (1cm) seam allowance and reverse stitching at each start and finish (see page 115). Trim the corners so they are flush with the straight sides of the tie. Open out the tie and press the seams open (see page 117).

**4** With the right sides of the fabrics together, place the two lining pieces onto the ends of the tie, matching up the raw edges. Sew down the sides of the lining pieces, pivoting at the corners (see page 116) so that the ⅜in (1cm) seam allowance stays constant all the way around. Reverse stitch at each start and finish. Trim the corners. If your fabric is delicate and likely to fray, reinforce your stitches by sewing over your original stitches by 1⅛in (3cm) either side of each point (see page 119).

**5** Turn each end of the tie to the right side and point out each corner. Press the seams and make sure the lining does not peep round and show on the right side of the tie (see step 2 on page 123).

**6** Follow steps 1–2 on page 128 (for making a tube strap) with the fabric for the keeper loop. You don't need to topstitch along each side.

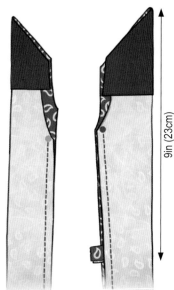

**7** Fold the tie in half along its width with the right sides together and match up the raw edges. Pin or fabric-clip down the long side. Fold the keeper loop piece in half and insert it between the two layers of the tie, 9in (23cm) up from the tip of the wider (front) end of the tie. Pin or fabric-clip the keeper loop in place, with ⅜in (1cm) of its raw edges sticking out from the raw edges of the tie. Sew along the raw long edge of the tie, reverse stitching at the start and finish. Sew as close as you can get to the lining at either end while keeping the seam allowance flat. The keeper loop will be sewn in place as you sew along the raw long edge of the tie.

**8** Press the seam open, making sure that it is in the center of the tie. Fix a safety pin on the narrower end of the tie in a place where any pulling won't rip the fabric. Dive down inside the tie with your safety pin and push the tip of the tie down inside too, following the pin. Feed the safety pin through the fabric tube and along to the other end. Release the bunched-up gathers every so often as you push the safety pin through so that you can continue.

*Tips*  The three pieces that make up this tie don't all need to be cut from the same fabric, so mix and match from your fabric stash and give yourself a surprise!

When cutting out and using delicate fabrics where pin pricks may mark the fabric, always place pins within the seam allowance.

You can make a tie out of any non-stretch fabric. If the fabric is a bit flimsy, you can reinforce it by ironing some fusible interfacing onto the back of the fabric before you start.

**9** Once you have turned the tie through to the right side, remove the safety pin and give your tie a good press so the seam lies centrally at the back. Hand-sew up the remaining gap at each end of the tie with whipstitch (see page 125). Keep your stitches small and make sure they don't show on the right side of the tie. Flatten down the keeper loop and sew some little stitches underneath each side of the loop where they won't be seen to keep the loop in place.

Skill level ✳✳✳

# Bucket Hat

The classic bucket hat is reinvented in this lovely bouclé fabric which is cozy and stylish. If you like the design, set your goals on a summer version in cotton!

**YOU WILL NEED**

Main fabric, 26 x 35½in (65 x 90cm)—I used bouclé
Lining fabric, 13¾ x 27½in (35 x 70cm)
Matching sewing thread
Basic sewing kit (see page 5)
Walking foot (optional but helpful with thick fabric)
Pressing ham

**FINISHED MEASUREMENTS**

Height of side: 2¾in (7cm), inner width: 8in (20cm)

**TEMPLATES REQUIRED (SEE PAGE 138)**

Crown
Side
Brim

**CUTTING GUIDE**

Cut 1 in each of the main fabric and lining fabric:
Crown

Cut 1 on fold in each of the main fabric and lining fabric:
Side

Cut 4 in the main fabric:
Brim

**LEARN HOW TO**

■ Sew different curves together
■ Handle stretchy fabric
■ Ease fabric in as you sew
■ Make a lining
■ Clip into curves
■ Sew a full circle

*Tips* The hat pattern is in a medium/large size with deep sides and brim, just how a bucket hat should be!

You can enlarge or decrease the size of the templates using a photocopier. Even a change of ³⁄₁₆in (0.5cm) can make a big difference to the size. Make up a sample using scrap fabric or an old bedsheet to check the fit.

Using a slightly stretchy fabric like this bouclé (which is a soft curly, looped fabric with a little one-way stretch) or a fleece fabric will make it easier to sew around the curves.

If your hat is going to be a bit floppy, you can reinforce the whole hat or just the brim with iron-on interfacing.

**1** Transfer the half point notches from the crown template to the wrong side of the main fabric crown piece with pen dots (see page 113). Also transfer the side piece's notches to the wrong side of both the main and lining fabric side pieces with pen dots. Fold the main side piece so its short sides are together and the right sides of the fabric are touching. Pin and sew down the short side, reverse stitching at the start and finish (see page 115). Repeat with the lining piece. Press the seams open (see page 117).

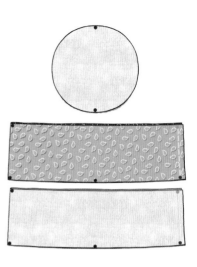

**2** With the right sides of the fabrics together, place the main-fabric crown piece onto the narrower side of the main-fabric side piece (the hat slightly tapers up to the crown). Match up the notches and secure the pieces together with pins at right angles to the top edge. Make sure the side seam is pressed open. Start from anywhere and sew on the side piece side, so you can see any tucks likely to happen (see tip below). Overlap your stitches by ³⁄₈in (1cm) when you get round to the beginning (see page 115). Take your time—you can always unpick the odd tuck and resew it. Repeat this step to sew the lining crown and lining side piece together. In the lining, any tucks may not matter so much, as long they're not distorting the shape of the hat.

*Tip* As you sew in step 2, it might look like that there is excess fabric in the side piece compared to the crown. You are placing two different curves together, so although they look like they won't fit together perfectly, you must ease (stretch gently) the fabrics together as you slowly sew round so they do fit. This is easier if the fabric has a slight stretch but can be done with cottons. Stretch the fabric of the side piece a little as you go round, pulling it slightly when the needle is down to make the two layers the same length, and continue sewing while keeping the tension.

**3** To reduce the bulkiness of the seam, trim one layer of the seam so that it is shorter than the other but is not less than ³⁄₁₆in (0.5cm) (see page 119). Then clip into the curves about every 1³⁄₁₆in (3cm) through both layers. Repeat with the hat lining. Turn the main-fabric piece right side out. If your fabric can be ironed, press the seam toward the side piece on the inside. A pressing ham can help you here.

**4** Mark the half-point notches with a pen dot and with the right sides touching, place two of the brim pieces together. Pin and then sew down each short side, reverse stitching at the start and finish. Repeat with the other two brim pieces. Press the seams open.

**5** Matching the notches and seams, place the narrower side of one brim onto the open end of the main-fabric hat with the right sides of the fabrics touching. Pin in place at right angles to the raw edge, or fabric-clip it in place. Repeat to pin or fabric-clip the other brim to the lining hat. Starting anywhere, sew steadily around on the brim side, easing in any excess fabric with a little stretch and by stopping often with the needle down to rearrange the fabric. Overlap your stitches by ⅜in (1cm) when you get back to the beginning. Repeat to sew the other brim to the lining hat.

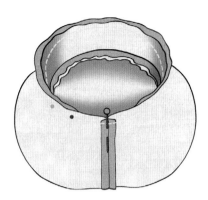

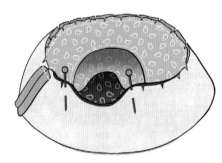

**6** In the hat lining, unpick (see page 117) 4in (10cm) along the seam between the brim and the side, to create a turning gap. As this area was previously sewn, it will make the sewing up of the turning gap in the curved brim easier when this is done later. Clip into the seam every 1¼in (3cm) all around the seam between the brim and the side on both the main and lining hats.

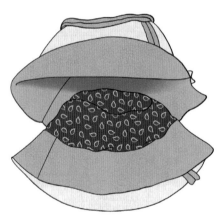

**7** Turn the lining hat to the right side and put it inside the main hat so their right sides are touching.

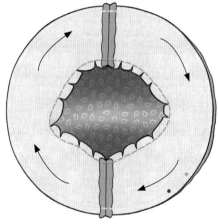

**8** Match the outer edges of the brims together and pin or fabric-clip them in place. Sew clockwise all around the edge, starting anywhere and overlapping your stitches by ⅜in (1cm) when you get back to the beginning.

**9** Layer the seam you have just sewn in the previous step by trimming one side shorter than the other (but so that it is not less than ³⁄₁₆in/0.5cm). Clip into the seam all the way round, with the snips about 1¼in (3cm) apart. Turn the hat to the right side by pulling the fabric out through the turning gap.

**10** Tuck the seam allowance of the turning gap to the wrong side and pin in place (see page 122). Use small whipstitches (see page 125) to hand-sew up the gap. Push the lining inside the main hat and press the hat well, making sure the brim seam is even all the way around. You can use a pressing ham inside the crown to help you press the tricky shape. Bucket hats are officially back! Packable and lightweight, they are perfect for all seasons.

Skill level ✳

Whether for city shopping, groceries, or days off browsing, we all need an attractive bag that can hold everything. With this reversible design, you can choose a side to match your outfit or mood. Plus, it has two big pockets that are perfect for storing your wallet or keys.

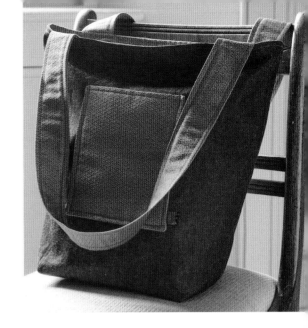

# Reversible Tote Bag

## YOU WILL NEED

Fabric A (red), 39½ x 45¼in (100 x 115cm) (see tip below. I used a twill weave cotton/polyester mix)

Fabric B (black denim), 31½ x 45¼in (80 x 115cm)

Sewing thread in complementary color

Basic sewing kit (see page 5)

Graph paper and/or set square

## TEMPLATE REQUIRED (SEE PAGE 136)

Reversible Tote Bag

## CUTTING GUIDE

Cut 2 of each of the following in fabric A and fabric B:

Reversible tote bag template (see step 1)

Pocket: rectangle measuring 7⅛ x 8¼in (18 x 21cm)

Cut 1 in each of fabric A and fabric B:

Pocket tab (optional): rectangle measuring 1⅝ x 4in (4 x 10cm)—cut from the selvage edge of the fabric (see page 112) if you would like to use the selvage as a feature on your tabs

Cut 2 in fabric A:

Straps: rectangle measuring 5⅛ x 31½in (13 x 80cm)

## FINISHED MEASUREMENTS

Bag: 18⅛in (46cm) wide at top, 15in (38cm) tall

Straps: 28¾in (73cm)

## LEARN HOW TO

- Draft up a paper pattern
- Sew tube straps
- Make boxed corners and match up the seams
- Make a patch pocket
- Sew a straight stitch and a zigzag stitch

**1** Using the instructions and the diagram on page 136, draft out the main body template on a piece of paper and cut it out. Use this template to cut out the main body pieces from your fabrics. Transfer the notches that are 2¾in (7cm) in from the top of each side onto the fabric A main body piece only (see page 112).

**2** Follow steps 1–3 (making a tube strap) on page 128 with each of the strap pieces. In step 1, use the right-hand side of your sewing-machine foot as your guide (see page 118) on the long raw edge of the fabric, and then trim the seam in half. After you have pressed the strap in step 3, topstitch (see page 114) down each long side, using the right-hand side of the sewing-machine foot as your guide on the edge of the fabric. You can either use thread that matches your fabric well or make a bold statement and use a contrasting thread color.

**3** To make the pocket tabs (optional), follow steps 1–3 on page 128 (for making a tube strap) with each of the fabric tab pieces. Alternatively, you can use the attractive fluffy selvage edge (see page 112) as a feature on the pocket tabs. Fold the lower edge of the tab piece toward the wrong side of the fabric, so that it comes just below the fluffy selvage edge (a). Fold the tab in half along its length and pin it in place. With the tab still folded, stitch around the three sides, leaving the short raw edge unsewn (b).

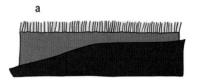

*Tip* So that the two sides of the bag will fit inside each other snugly, try to use fabrics that are the same type and weight.

**4** Lay two matching pocket pieces together with the right sides touching. Follow steps 1–2 on page 123 to make a patch pocket. In step 1, leave a 4in (10cm) turning gap in the bottom edge. Repeat with the other two matching pocket pieces.

**5** Place the fabric A main body piece on the table with the right side of the fabric facing upward. Position the fabric B pocket in the center of the main body piece, 4in (10cm) down from the top edge (or you can choose your own position). Tuck the fabric B pocket tab under the bottom right-hand side of the pocket, so that the raw edges of the tab go underneath the pocket by ⅜in (1cm). Pin the pocket and the tab in place. Using the right-hand side of the sewing-machine foot as your guide on the edge of the pocket, topstitch around the three lower sides, reverse stitching at the start and finish (see step 3 on page 123). Sew carefully over the tab. Repeat to sew the fabric A pocket onto the fabric B main body piece.

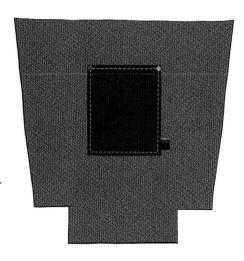

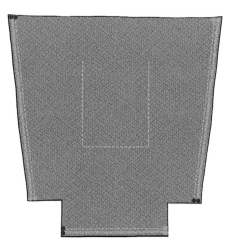

**6** Place the two fabric A main body pieces together with the right sides touching. Match up the edges and pin together. Sew down each side and along the bottom edge, using a ⅝in (1.5cm) seam allowance. To help you, you can use a ruler and a pen or chalk marker to draw straight lines and then sew directly on top of these lines. Don't sew along the cut-out corners.

To reinforce the seam, sew a line of zigzag stitching in between each stitch line and the edge of the fabric (see page 119). Repeat with the fabric B main body pieces but leave a 4in (10cm) turning gap in the bottom edge (see page 122). Please note that the turning gap can be left in either of the main body pieces—choose the one less likely to fray.

**7** To make a boxed corner, take hold of a bottom corner on the fabric A bag piece from the inside, and place the right sides of the corner together. To match up the seams, place a pin through the stitch line in the bottom of the bag and line it up with the stitch line on the side of the bag (see page 120). Flatten out the corner. Draw a line across the corner, ⅝in (1.5cm) away

from the raw edge. The line will be about 6¼in (16cm) long. Pin in place and then sew on this drawn line, reverse stitching at the start and finish. Sew a line of zigzag stitches to reinforce the seam. Repeat with the second bottom corner of the fabric A bag, and then with the two bottom corners of the fabric B bag.

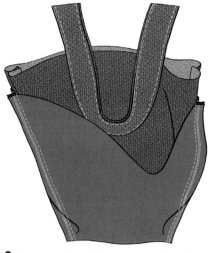

**9** Match the outside edge of each end of the strap to the markings on the top of the fabric A main body piece. Pin the strap ends in place so that they extend above the top raw edge of the fabric A bag by ⅜in (1cm). Repeat to pin the second strap in between the fabrics on the other side of the bag. Use a pin to match up the side seams at the top of the bag, then match up the edges of fabric A and fabric B all around the top and pin them together. Using a ⅜in (1cm) seam allowance, sew all the way around the top, starting at a side seam and sewing over the straps as you go. When you get back to where you started, overlap your stitches (see page 115) by ⅜in (1cm).

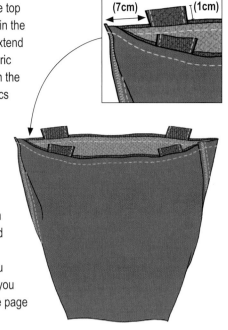

2¾in (7cm)    ⅜in (1cm)

**8** Turn the fabric A bag so the right side of the fabric is on the outside. Place it inside the fabric B bag, so the right sides of the fabrics are touching. Place one of the straps in between the fabric A and fabric B layers on one side of the bag. Make sure the strap is not twisted and the seam side of the strap faces inward.

**10** To turn the bag to the right side, pull the right side of the fabric out through the 4in (10cm) opening in the bottom edge.

**11** Once pulled through, tuck under the raw edges of the 4in (10cm) opening and pin them together. Sew up the opening (see page 122), using the right-hand side of the sewing-machine foot as your guide on the edge of the fabric. Reverse stitch at the start and finish.

**12** Push one side of the bag inside the other. Give the bag a good press around the top, making sure that neither fabric is peeping out above the other. Using the same spool and bobbin thread that you used for the straps, topstitch all the way around the top of the bag, starting from one of the side seams. Use the right-hand side of the sewing-machine foot as your guide on the edge of the fabric. This topstitching will in turn reinforce the straps as you sew over them. When you get round to where you started, overlap your stitches by ⅜in (1cm). Now where's your purse? You're ready to hit the shops!

Revamp any bag with this impressive adjustable strap. This is a great project for using up spare pieces of fabric, and you could create several statement straps to suit different outfits.

# Bag Strap

**1** I used the full width of my fabric and so by using the selvage (see page 112) at each end, I didn't have raw edges to finish on the short ends. If you have raw edges at the short ends of your strap fabric, fold each short end to the wrong side of the fabric by ⅜in (1cm) and press (see page 117). This will make neat tucked-in edges when you turn the strap through to the right side.

## YOU WILL NEED

Main fabric, 5½ x 55in (14 x 140cm) (choose a sturdy fabric without any stretch such as cotton, a cotton/polyester mix, denim, or linen)

Medium-weight iron-on interfacing, 5½ x 55in (14 x 140cm) (you will need to cut the interfacing in two or three pieces—just butt up the edges of the pieces when you iron them onto the strap fabric in step 1)

Matching sewing thread

1 x 2¼in (6cm) wide tri-glide slide (this allows you to have an adjustable strap)

2 x 2¼in (6cm) wide swivel clasps

Basic sewing kit (see page 5)

Zipper foot

## FINISHED MEASUREMENTS

2 x 48½in (5 x 123cm)

## LEARN HOW TO

- Make a long tube strap and turn it through
- Use iron-on interfacing
- Sew through thick fabric
- Use a zipper foot

**2** Iron the interfacing onto the wrong side of the main fabric. Then follow step 1 on page 129 (making a folded strap). Trim the seam if the fabric is thick (see page 119) and set the seam with an iron (see page 117).

**3** Turn the strap through to the right side—see page 128 for different ways you can do this. I used a safety pin to help me because the fabric wasn't too bulky.

**4** Use your fingers to roll out the seam so that it can be seen at one side edge of the strap and it is not tucked in (see page 120). Press the strap. Topstitch along both long sides of the strap (see step 3 on page 128), using the right-hand side of the sewing-machine foot on as your guide on the edge of the fabric (see page 118). Reverse stitch at the start and finish (see page 115). Choose which side of the strap you want to be the right side, then fold each end of the strap toward the the same side by 1½in (4cm) and press.

**5** Slip one end of the strap around the middle bar of the tri-glide slider, so that the middle bar sits in the fold near the end of the strap.

**6** Put the zipper foot on your sewing machine (see page 130). Sew across the strap close to the slider, reverse stitching at the start and finish. Using the zipper foot allows you to sew close to the slider. You can reinforce this with another line of stitching close to the first line.

**7** Thread the free end of the strap through one of the swivel clasps. Then thread the free end into one side of the tri-glide slider, over the middle bar of the slider, and through the other side of the slider.

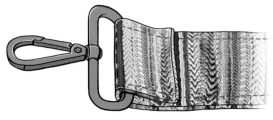

**8** Loop the free end of the strap around the second swivel clasp. Fold this end of the strap back along the crease where it has already been pressed. Using the zipper foot, sew this end of the strap in place as you did with the slider, reverse stitching at the start and finish. You can reinforce this with another line of stitching close to the first line. The fabric may be thick here so you might need to do some handwheel stitches to help you sew through the layers (see page 115). Now where's that bag? You're ready to go out and show off your new strap! And if you haven't got a suitable bag, you can make one (see page 74).

*Tips* You could take the swivel clasps and buckle from an old bag or belt.

If you are using striped fabric, make sure the stripes match up along the seam.

Fabric widths can vary from dress fabrics that are 45¼in (115cm) wide to soft furnishing or sheeting that are 55in (140cm) wide. If you need to make the strap in two pieces, add ⅜in (1cm) to a short side of each piece to allow for a seam. Sew the

pieces together using a ⅜in (1cm) seam allowance, and press the seam open (see page 117). You could also make a patch strap from smaller scraps of fabric—again, add ⅜in (1cm) to each piece, sew the pieces together, and press the seams open.

An everyday essential, this purse is perfect for storing cards, coins, or small make-up items. Its size makes it easy to slip into a small bag or coat pocket.

Skill level ✳✳

# Foldable Coin Purse

## YOU WILL NEED

Main fabric, 12 x 12in (30 x 30cm)

Lining fabric, 12 x 12in (30 x 30cm)

Fusible fleece (optional, for stability and/or quilting), 12 x 12in (30 x 30cm)

Matching sewing thread

Narrow cord or strip of elastic, ⅛in (3mm) wide and 3⅛in (8cm) long

Button

Basic sewing kit (see page 5)

Fabric clips

Pointer

## FINISHED MEASUREMENTS

4 x 5½in (10 x 14cm)

## TEMPLATE REQUIRED
## (SEE PAGE 135)

Foldable Coin Purse sewing guide

## LEARN HOW TO

■ Use a sewing guide template

■ Sew curves and corners

■ Clip curves and corners

■ Leave a turning gap

■ Topstitch the purse together

■ Sew on a button

*Tips* You will sew through thick layers, so omit the fusible fleece if it adds too much thickness to the layers.

You can quilt the square of main fabric (see page 127) before you cut out the template for extra texture.

For the elastic, I used a small piece of elastic cord from a chocolate box as you don't need much!

**1** Iron the fusible fleece (if using) onto the wrong side of the main fabric. You can quilt this square for added effect (see page 127). Fold the lining piece in half and press (see page 117), then open the piece out again. Place the main fabric and lining fabric together with the right sides touching.

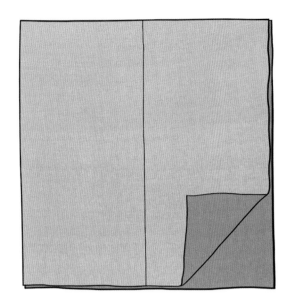

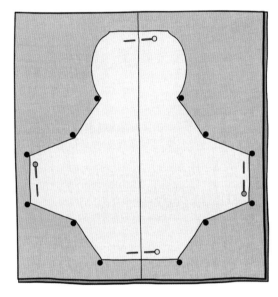

**2** Place the template on top of the fabrics, matching up its center line with the pressed crease in the lining. This ensures that the grainline (see page 112) is straight on your purse. Using a pen, draw around the rounded flap at the top. For the rest of the shape, you can mark the points of all the corners with a dot, then remove the template and join up the dots with a ruler and pen.

**3** Mark a turning gap (see page 122) of 2¾in (7cm) at the top of the flap by placing two pins into the fabric at right angles to the top of the flap. Also pin the fabric together around the lower part of the shape. Starting at one side of the turning gap, sew all the way round the shape on top of your drawn line, until you get to the other side of the turning gap. If your machine foot has a central gap, place the gap directly on the drawn line to guide you. Pivot (see page 116) at all the angles to get accurate corners, and reverse stitch at the start and finish (see page 115). Trim the seam allowance to ⅜in (1cm) along the turning gap, and ¼in (6mm) all the way around the rest of the shape. Clip the curves around the flap and clip the corners (see page 119), being careful not to snip through your stitches.

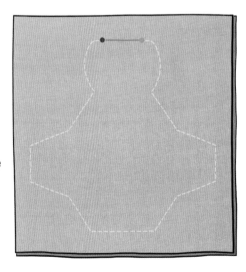

**4** Pull the right side of the fabric out through the turning gap to turn the coin purse through to the right side. It may be tricky if the fabric is thick, but alternate between pushing the wrong side of the fabric into the gap and pulling the right side out of the gap.

**5** Push out all the corners and curves with a pointer and give the fabric a good press. Tuck in the raw edges of the turning gap evenly and neatly.

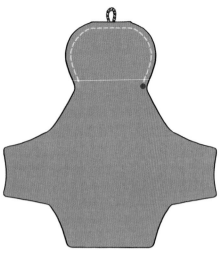

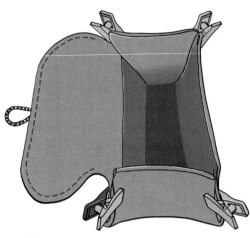

**6** Measure where the center of the top edge of the flap is, and place a pin in the fabric there. Fold the piece of elastic in half to make a loop. Tuck the loop ends in between the two layers of fabric at the center of the top of the flap, and fix the elastic in place with a pin or a fabric clip. Make sure that the elastic loop will fit over your button, and adjust the length of the loop if necessary. Using the right-hand side of the sewing-machine foot as your guide (see page 118) on the edge of the fabric, topstitch (see page 114) neatly around the flap, securing the loop in place as you sew. Reverse stitch at the start and finish.

**7** Bring the sides of the coin purse together, matching up all the edges. Fabric-clip the sides in place.

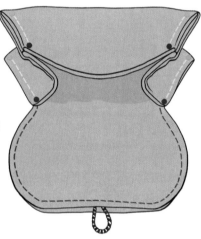

**8** Starting from the bottom of the purse, topstitch along one of the sides, using the right-hand side of your sewing-machine foot as your guide on the edge of the fabric. Reverse stitch at the start and finish. Repeat with the other three sides. You may find that the layers are quite thick, so take it slowly especially when you are reverse stitching.

**9** When you have stitched all four sides, press each seams. Sew a button onto the front of the coin purse (see page 129), making sure that the button is positioned so that the elastic loop will fit around it easily. No more looking for loose change—this accessory will keep everything organized!

We all get caught out without a tote or with one that's not big enough sometimes, but this roomy bag won't let you down! As it folds away neatly, you easily can tuck it into a purse (handbag) or pocket so you'll always have it to hand.

# Foldaway Tote

## YOU WILL NEED

**For the main bag:** 2 pieces of fabric (choose a lightweight fabric such as cotton lawn), each 18⅛ x 18⅛in (46 x 46cm)

**For the straps:** 4 pieces of fabric, each 2¾ x 23⅝in (7 x 60cm)

**For the pocket:** fabric, 6¾ x 15in (17 x 38cm)

Matching sewing thread
Basic sewing kit (see page 5)
Pointer

## FINISHED MEASUREMENTS

15¾ x 17in (40 x 43cm)

## LEARN HOW TO

- Sew a double hem
- Make tube straps
- Construct a pocket
- Topstitch along the bag top

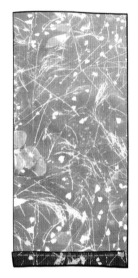

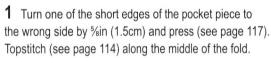

**1** Turn one of the short edges of the pocket piece to the wrong side by ⅝in (1.5cm) and press (see page 117). Topstitch (see page 114) along the middle of the fold.

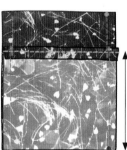

5½in (14cm)

**2** Turn the pocket piece over so the right side of the fabric is facing upward. Fold the side with the sewn hem up by 5½in (14cm), with the right sides of the fabric together. Pin down the sides. Sew down each side with a ⅝in (1.5cm) seam allowance. Reverse stitch (see page 115) for a few stitches over the folded hem to reinforce it before continuing to the end. Reverse stitch at the bottom of the pocket, but it's not necessary to reverse stitch at the top because this side is going to be sewn into a seam.

**3** Turn the pocket to the right side and use a pointer to point out the corners. Press the pocket so the sides at the top are folded to the wrong side by ⅝in (1.5cm).

*Tips* The fabric needs to be lightweight, strong, and foldable. Cotton lawn is a good choice as it's not as slippery to sew as polyester.

Old shower curtains would also work well and come in lots of bright and fun designs.

Lightweight fabric can get caught up in the feed dogs of your sewing machine, so always start a little farther in to the edge of the fabric than you would normally to allow the feed dogs enough to grip on to.

**4** Press a double hem (see page 121) on the top edge (if it's obvious as with a directional print, see page 113) of both main pieces. On the wrong side of one of the main pieces, find the center of the folded edge by folding the piece in half and marking it with a pin. Do the same to fold the pocket in half and mark the center with a pin at the top of the pocket. Tuck the top raw edge of the pocket underneath the double hem of the main bag, matching up the two pins so the pocket is positioned in the center. Pin or fabric-clip the pocket in place.

**5** Place two of the strap pieces together with their right sides touching. Pin down each long side, close to the raw edges. Sew down each long side of the strap, reverse stitching at the start and finish. Repeat with the second two strap pieces.

**6** Using a safety pin, turn each of the straps to the right side (see page 128). Press the straps so that the seams are positioned at the outer edges (see page 120).

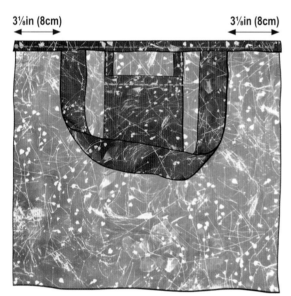

3⅛in (8cm)            3⅛in (8cm)

**7** Lay a strap on the wrong side of the main piece that has the pocket attached. Tuck the strap ends under the top hem either side of the pocket, making sure the strap is not twisted. Position the strap ends 3⅛in (8cm) away from each side of the main piece. Pin or fabric-clip the straps in place. On the wrong side of the main bag piece, topstitch in the middle of the double hem, sewing over the strap ends and the top of the pocket. Reverse stitch at the start and finish. Make sure your bobbin thread matches your fabric well. Repeat to sew the second strap into the double hem on the other main piece, again positioning the strap ends so that they are 3⅛in (8cm) away from each side of the main piece.

**8** To make the strap lie in the right direction, flip it up so it folds back on itself and fabric-clip it in place. On the wrong side of the main piece, topstitch along the double hem again, but parallel to your first row of stitching and about ⅛in (3mm) away from it. This will also reinforce your straps. Make sure your pocket is pinned out of the way, so it doesn't get caught up in your stitches.

**9** Place the two main bag pieces together with the right sides touching. Pin along the sides and along the bottom, making sure they meet perfectly and are level at the top of the double hems. Sew along the three sides with a ⅝in (1.5cm) seam allowance, reverse stitching at the start and finish. In between the row of straight stitching and the raw edge of the fabric, zigzag stitch (see page 114) all around the three sides of the bag. When you sew the two outside corners in zigzag stitch, make sure the needle is in the right-hand position when you leave it down and pivot (see page 116), so you get a neater zigzag stitch at each corner.

**10** Trim along the sides and bottom edge, close to the zigzag stitching (see page 119). Press the seams to set them (see page 117), then turn the bag to the right side. Use a pointer to point out the corners, then press the bag.

**11** The following steps show how to fold the bag up into its pocket. Have the side of the bag without the pocket facing upward and flip the pocket so that it is sticking out at the top. Fold the straps down onto the bag and then fold in the left-hand side of the bag.

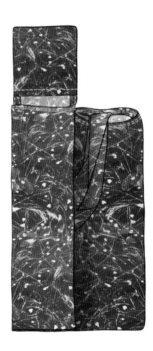

**12** Fold in the right-hand side of the bag.

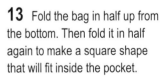

**13** Fold the bag in half up from the bottom. Then fold it in half again to make a square shape that will fit inside the pocket.

**14** Push the folded bag into the pocket. Now you'll always have a bag handy and never be caught out clutching your purchases in your arms again. Let the shopping begin!

# Glasses/Phone Case

This is the perfect design to store your specs, sunnies, or smartphone, keeping them safe and cozy in a padded pouch. The case has side tabs for a strap and a secure magnetic closure. With many purposes, this project makes a great gift.

## YOU WILL NEED

**For the main case:** two pieces of fabric, each 5⅛ x 6¾in (13 x 17cm)

**For the lining:** two pieces of contrast fabric, each 5⅛ x 9⅞in (13 x 25cm)

**For the side loops (optional):** fabric, 2 x 4¾in (5 x 12cm)

Two pieces of fusible fleece, each 5⅛ x 9in (13 x 23cm)

Matching sewing thread

Magnetic clasp

Basic sewing kit (see page 5)

Pointer

## FINISHED MEASUREMENTS

4 x 7½in (10 x 19cm)

## TEMPLATE REQUIRED
## (SEE PAGE 135)

Case template

## LEARN HOW TO

■ Create a lining
■ Topstitch for a professional finish
■ Attach a magnetic clasp
■ Make side loops

*Tips* To make a custom case for a device, just measure your device and add 1in (2.5cm) to the measurements on each side.

Make a matching key fob wristlet (see page 42).

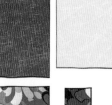

**1** Once you have cut out all the pieces following the template, mark a central dot 2¾in (7cm) down from one of the short sides on each of the lining pieces as noted on the template. This is to mark where the two sides of the magnetic clasp will go.

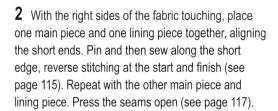

**2** With the right sides of the fabric touching, place one main piece and one lining piece together, aligning the short ends. Pin and then sew along the short edge, reverse stitching at the start and finish (see page 115). Repeat with the other main piece and lining piece. Press the seams open (see page 117).

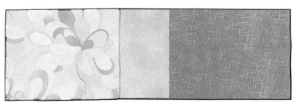

**3** Iron a piece of fusible fleece onto the wrong side of one of the stitched-together pieces, covering the seam so all the main fabric and only part of the lining is covered by the fleece. Repeat with the other piece.

**4** Topstitch (see page 114) down either side of the seam on the right side of the fabric. Start sewing both rows from the same side and use the side of the sewing-machine foot on the seam as your guide for both (see page 118), so the rows are parallel. Take the guard disc part of the magnetic clasp and match up its central hole with the dot you made on the lining. Mark the fabric with a pen through the two slits either side of the dot. Attach a side of the magnetic clasp each of the lining pieces (see page 131).

**5** Take the fabric piece for the side loop and follow steps 1–2 on page 129 (making a folded strap). Topstitch close to the edge down both sides (see page 114). Cut the strap in half. Fabric-clip the side loops onto the sides of the case with the loops facing inward and positioned so they are next to the seam with their ends flush to the raw edge. Place the other case side on top so right sides of the fabrics are touching and the tab loops are sandwiched in between.

**6** Match up all the raw edges and also match up the seams with a pin (see page 120). Pin all the way around, leaving a 3⅛in (8cm) turning gap in the short edge of the lining. Mark the turning gap with two pins placed at right angles to the short edge. Sew all the way around, leaving the turning gap unsewn and reverse stitching at the start and finish. Sew carefully over the tabs as the layers will be thick. You may need to use some handwheel stitches and pull it through gently from the back (see page 115).

**7** Trim the seams and cut off the corners (see page 119). Turn the case through to the right side by pulling and pushing the fabric out through the turning gap. Once it is through to the right side, give the case a press. Tuck in the raw edges of the seam allowance at the turning gap. Pin it in place and sew up the gap (see page 122).

**8** Push the lining into the main case and use a pointer to get the corners of the lining right into corners of the main case. About 1½in (4cm) of the lining should be showing. Protecting your phone's screen or your lenses from everyday bumps and scratches is important, so it makes sense they have their own soft padded sleeping bag!

Why carry your bag when you can wear it? This crossbody bag can accommodate all your everyday essentials with ease and its practical design includes an internal zippered pocket to keep your valuables secure.

# Crossbody Bag

## YOU WILL NEED

**For the main bag:** main fabric (denim, linen, corduroy, tweed, soft-furnishing fabrics, or quilting cotton reinforced with iron-on interfacing would all work well), 19¾ x 19¾in (50 x 50cm)

**For the strap:** main fabric, 3⅛ x 44⅛in (8 x 112cm) (this can be cut out in two pieces)

**For the strap tabs:** 2 pieces of main fabric, each 3⅛ x 4in (8 x 10cm)

**For the lining:** lining fabric (such as quilting cotton), 19¾ x 19¾in (50 x 50cm)

**For the internal pocket:** lining fabric, 10¼ x 15¾in (26 x 40cm)

Matching sewing thread
8in (20cm) nylon zipper for internal pocket
16n (40cm) nylon zipper for main opening
1 x 1½in- (4cm-)wide tri-glide slide buckle
2 x 1½in- (4cm-)wide D-rings or rectangular rings
Basic sewing kit (see page 5)
Quilter's tape/double-sided tape

## FINISHED MEASUREMENTS

Bag: 8 x 17in (20 x 43cm)
Strap length: 44in (112cm)

## TEMPLATES REQUIRED (SEE PAGE 141)

Front
Back
Lining Back
Letterbox Internal Pocket

## CUTTING GUIDE

Cut 1 of the following in each of the main fabric and lining fabric:
Front

Cut 1 of the following in the main fabric:
Back

Cut 1 of each of the following in the lining fabric:
Lining Back
Letterbox Internal Pocket

## LEARN HOW TO

- Sew a zipper
- Create a letterbox opening
- Hand-sew a lining in place
- Make tube straps with a buckle

**1** Mark the central notches on the front, back, and lining back pieces as per the templates with chalk or a pen dot. Also mark the side notches on the right side of the main-fabric back piece.

**2** Using the template, mark the center on the wrong side of the letterbox internal pocket piece. Also transfer the thin rectangle onto the wrong side of the letterbox pocket, using the "pin and mark" method on the corners (see page 113). Then use a ruler and a pen or chalk marker to join up the dots to draw the rectangle. Inside the rectangle, mark the central line and "V" shapes at each end.

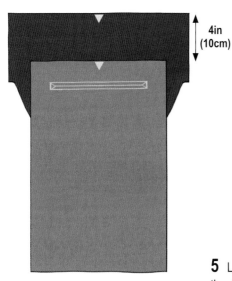

**4in (10cm)**

**3** Place the pocket 4in (10cm) down from the top of the lining back piece with the right sides of the fabrics touching. Align both center markings so the pocket is in the center. Follow steps 2–6 on pages 130–131 to sew the internal pocket, with the 8in (20cm) nylon zipper. When you flip up the pocket to meet the top raw edge, pin then sew around the three raw-edged sides, making sure you're only sewing the pocket piece and not through to the lining.

**4** Press (see page 117) the top straight edges of the lining front and lining back pieces to the wrong side by ⅜in (1cm). Sew these edges in place using the right-hand side of the foot as your guide on the folded edge of the fabric (see page 118).

**5** Lay the lining front onto the lining back piece with the right sides together, matching the curved edges. Pin and then sew round the curve over the top of the lining front's hem and through the internal pocket that is beneath the lining back. Reverse stitch at the start and finish (see page 115). Trim away the excess internal pocket fabric.

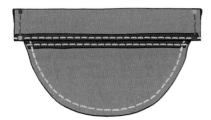

**6** Fold the top edge of the lining back down to meet the pressed edge of the lining front. Pin in place at both sides. Sew down each side, reverse stitching at the start and finish.

**7** Lay the 16in (40cm) nylon zipper right side down onto the main front piece with the right sides touching. It is okay if the zipper is longer than the main piece. If it's an open-ended zipper, put a fabric clip or pin on each end of the zipper so the zipper pull doesn't accidentally slide off. With a zipper foot on your sewing machine (see page 130), sew along the zipper tape about ³⁄₁₆in (0.5cm) away from the teeth, reverse stitching at the start and finish. You may be able to put the right-hand side of your zipper foot on the edge of the zipper tape to guide you, if the zipper foot is the right width. Move the zipper pull out of the way if necessary by leaving your needle in, lifting your sewing-machine foot, and sliding the pull away. Then put your sewing machine foot and needle down again and continue sewing. Mark the center of the zipper on the free long edge of the zipper tape.

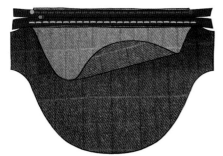

**8** Fold the main front piece away from the zipper. Lay the other long edge of the zipper on the main back piece with the right sides touching, matching up the central marks. Pin and then sew along the other side of the zipper tape about ³⁄₁₆in (0.5cm) away from the teeth. Reverse stitch at the start and finish.

**9** Fold the front piece away from the zipper so the right sides of both pieces are facing upward. Press the two seams away from the zipper teeth, being careful not to get too near the nylon zipper teeth with the heat. Topstitch (see page 114) down each side about ³⁄₁₆in (0.5cm) from the edge with the zipper foot on your sewing machine.

**10** Take one of the strap tab pieces and follow steps 1–3 on page 128 to make a tube strap. In step 3, topstitch down each side using the right-hand side of the sewing-machine foot as your guide on the edge of the fabric. Repeat with the second strap tab piece.

**11** If you have cut out your strap in two pieces, sew the short ends together and then press the seam open. Press each short end of the strap to the wrong side by ³⁄₈in (1cm). Then fold the strap in half along its length with the right sides together and pin down its length. Sew down the long raw edge, sewing over the folded edges at either end, too (see page 129). Reverse stitch at the start and finish.

**12** Turn the strap through to the right side using a safety pin (see page 128). Press the strap with the the seam at the side (see page 120) and the folded short ends neatly tucked in. Topstitch down each long side using the right-hand side of the sewing-machine foot as your guide on the edge of the strap.

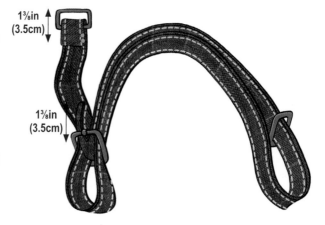

1³⁄₈in (3.5cm)

1³⁄₈in (3.5cm)

**13** Put one end of the strap through the D ring/rectangular ring. Fold the end of the strap over by 1³⁄₈in (3.5cm), and fabric-clip in place. Topstitch across the end of the strap to secure the D-ring/rectangular ring in place. Sew about ³⁄₈in (1cm) away from the strap end so you don't sew through the bulky seam. Sew a second row parallel to the first for extra strength. Thread the free end of the strap in and out of the two sides of the slide buckle. Thread the second D-ring/rectangular ring onto the free end of the strap. Take the free end of the strap and thread it around the middle bar of the slide buckle from underneath. Fabric-clip the strap in place so that it is folded over the middle bar of the slide buckle by 1³⁄₈in (3.5cm).

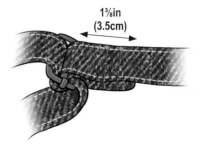

1³⁄₈in (3.5cm)

**14** Topstitch across the folded end of strap with two parallel lines of stitches.

**15** Fold a strap tab around the free side of one of the D rings/rectangular rings, so the raw edges of the tab are together. Within the seam allowance, sew across the raw edges of the strap tab to secure it. Repeat with the other strap tab.

**16** With the right side of the main bag uppermost, lay the strap tabs on either side of the main back piece. The upper side of each tab should be on each center mark. Position each tab at a right angle to the edge of the back piece with the loop facing inward and fabric-clip or pin in place. Starting from one strap tab and going across to the other, check that the strap isn't twisted and that the right side of the strap (check the buckle and D-rings) is touching the right side of the bag.

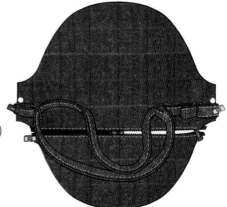

**17**  Open the zipper halfway. Flip the main back piece over the front piece so the right sides of the fabrics are touching and the zipper is hidden. Match up the curved raw edges and pin or fabric-clip them together all the way around. The strap tabs will be sandwiched at the sides between the folded main back piece, and you will sew over them to secure them in place. Make sure the strap is safely tucked inside and it isn't near the edge where you could sew over it. Turn the piece over so you are sewing on the side with the zipper. Sew all the way round the raw edges, making sure you keep the curved shape and that the two ends of the zipper tapes are together when you sew over them at the side. Reverse stitch at the start and finish.

**18**  Sew a row of zigzag stitching next to your row of straight stitching and near the raw edge, to reinforce the seam and prevent any fraying (see page 119). Trim the seam to the zigzag, clip into the curves (see page 119), and trim the ends of the zipper so it is flush with the edge of the bag.

**19**  Turn the bag to the right side through the zipper opening and press it, especially all around the front to make the curve smooth.

**20**  Turn the main bag inside out again. Turn the lining bag right side out. Measure and mark the center of each finished hem of the lining opening with a dot. Also mark the center of each long side of the zipper tape. Insert the main bag into the lining so the wrong side of the main bag is touching the wrong side of the lining. Match up the finished edges of the lining with the zipper tape, using your dot marks to get them central. Pin or fabric-clip the lining to the zipper tape so the lining is about ³⁄₁₆in (0.5cm) away from the zipper teeth. Whipstitch (see page 125) the lining onto each side of the zipper tape and as far up as you can at each side of the zipper.

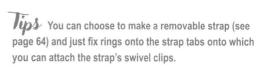

**21**  Turn the bag to the right side through the zipper opening and push the lining out to all the corners and sides inside the main bag. This accessory is a practical choice when you're on the move and want easy access to your things.

*Tips*  You can choose to make a removable strap (see page 64) and just fix rings onto the strap tabs onto which you can attach the strap's swivel clips.

You don't have to put a lining in—just omit steps 2–7 and step 21, but finish your inside seams neatly with a straight stitch and zigzag stitch.

# Plush Tote

Made in a super-soft fabric and with stuffed handles, this fluffy bag is a joy to carry. It has an internal zippered pocket, a magnetic clasp, and can easily fit your everyday kit of essentials.

## YOU WILL NEED

**For the outside:** 2 pieces of faux fur fabric, each 11 x 14¼in (28 x 36cm)

2 pieces of iron-on interfacing, each 11 x 14¼in (28 x 36cm)

**For the tab closure:** 2 pieces of faux fur fabric, each 7 x 3½in (17.5 x 8.5cm)

**For the lining:** 2 pieces of cotton fabric, each 11 x 14¼in (28 x 36cm)

2 pieces of fusible fleece, each 11 x 14¼in (28 x 36cm)

**For the letterbox internal pocket:** cotton/lining fabric, 10⅝ x 14¼in (27 x 36cm)

**For the straps:** 2 pieces of faux fur fabric, each 4 x 13¾in (10 x 35cm)

2 pieces of iron-on interfacing, each 4 x 13¾in (10 x 35cm)

**For the strap loops (optional):** 2 pieces of ribbon, each ⅜–¾cm (1–2cm) wide and 2½in (6cm) long

8in (20cm) nylon zipper

Magnetic clasp

Small amount of stuffing/fabric scraps to fill the straps

Matching sewing thread

Basic sewing kit (see page 5)

Knitting needle or chopstick

Quilter's tape

## FINISHED MEASUREMENTS

Bag: 9 x 13in (23 x 33cm)

Straps: 13¾in (35cm)

## TEMPLATES REQUIRED (SEE PAGE 142)

Letterbox Internal Pocket

Tab

## CUTTING GUIDE

Cut 1 of the following on the fold in the letterbox internal pocket lining fabric:

Letterbox Internal Pocket

Cut 2 of the following in the tab closure faux fur fabric:

Tab

## LEARN HOW TO

■ Sew with faux fur

■ Make tube straps

■ Create a letterbox zipped internal pocket

■ Construct an envelope-fold boxed corner

**1** Iron the fusible fleece to the wrong side of the lining pieces. Iron the interfacing to the wrong sides of the faux fur pieces and straps. Fold the faux fur outside pieces and lining pieces in half along the long side and mark the center at the top of each piece, on the right sides of the fabrics. The top of the outside bag piece is where the faux fur is flowing down from, so the direction of the faux fur (nap) should go toward the bottom of the bag. For the strap positions, mark two dots along the top on either side, 3⅛in (8cm) in from the side on the faux fur and the lining pieces.

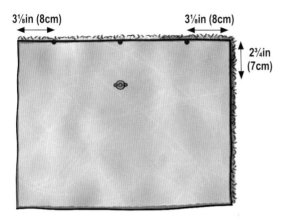
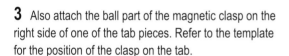

**2** To position the socket part of the magnetic clasp, on the back of one of the faux fur pieces, draw a dot in the center and 2¾in (7cm) down from the top edge. Mark and make the slits for the prongs (it may be easier to do this on the wrong side of the faux fur piece) and then insert the magnetic clasp from the right side (see page 131).

**3** Also attach the ball part of the magnetic clasp on the right side of one of the tab pieces. Refer to the template for the position of the clasp on the tab.

*Tips* When cutting out the faux fur fabric, make sure you follow the grainline of the faux fur so the direction of the fur (nap) will run down each piece and not diagonally.

Sewing and cutting faux fur will make a mess so be pre-warned, you will get covered in fluff!

Use a pin to tease out the faux fur that gets trapped in the seams.

As you sew along the faux fur seams, use the point of an unpicker or scissors to tuck any tufts back inside the seam.

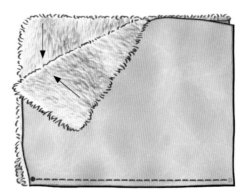

**4** With the right sides of the fabric together, pin or fabric-clip the two outside faux fur pieces together along the lower edge. Make sure the direction of fur (nap) is running down toward the lower edge. Sew along the lower edge, reverse stitching at the start and finish (see page 115). Reinforce this seam with zigzag stitching (see page 119), both for extra strength and to prevent any fur shedding. Trim along the seam. On the right side, use a pin to tease out any trapped fur in the seam.

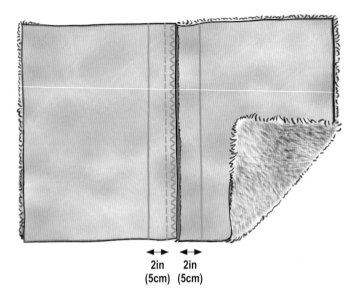

2in (5cm)  2in (5cm)

**5** Open out the outside pieces and place them on the table so the wrong side of the fabric is uppermost. Use a ruler and a chalk marker or pen to draw two parallel lines, each 2in (5cm) away from the central seam.

**6** With the right sides of the fabric together, fold along one of the drawn lines (you can press in the folds if your fabric can take the heat of an iron) and fabric-clip along the fold to keep it in place. Repeat with the other drawn line. Then bring the two fabric-clipped lines together and re-clip them together so the bottom seam is enclosed. From the side, it will look like an "M" shape (see step 5 on page 45 of the Reversible Notebook Cover project).

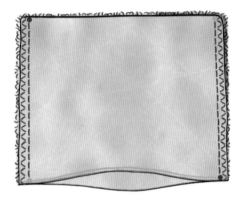

**7** With the right sides of the bag together, match up the raw edges. Fabric-clip or pin down each side. Sew down each side, reverse stitching at the start and finish. Zigzag-stitch along each edge to reinforce the seam.

**8** Take one of the pieces of faux fur fabric for the straps and follow steps 1–3 on page 128 to make a tube strap. Once you have turned it through to the right side, omit the topstitching and tease out any fluff caught in the seam. Repeat with the second strap piece.

**9** From both ends of one of the straps, gently push small amounts of stuffing inside the strap using a knitting needle or chopstick, to make a soft handle that can curve slightly. Keep any stuffing away from the ends of the strap. Repeat with the other strap.

**10** Place the tab pieces together with the right sides of the fabric touching. Pin and then sew all around the edge, leaving the bottom straight side unsewn. Reverse stitch at the start and finish. Clip into the curves (see page 119) and turn the tab through to the right side. Tease out any fur caught in the seam.

**11** Follow steps 1–6 on pages 130–131 to sew the letterbox internal pocket to one of the lining pieces.

**12** Follow steps 4–6 with the two lining pieces. With the right sides of the lining fabric together, match up the raw edges. Pin or fabric-clip down each short side, marking a turning gap of 4in (10cm) in one side with two pins at right angles to the edge of the fabric. Sew down each side, leaving the turning gap unsewn (see step 13 on page 95 of the Laptop Bag project). Reverse stitch at each start and finish.

**13** Turn the lining bag through to the right side. Take one of the straps and with its seam facing inward, pin or fabric-clip the raw ends of the strap on the marks that are 3⅛in (8cm) from each side of the lining bag. Repeat to pin or fabric-clip the other strap on the other side of the lining bag. Make sure the fur lies in the same direction on both straps. Position the tab in the middle, on the central mark and in between the two strap ends. The side of the tab with the magnetic clasp should be touching the right side of the lining. Optional: You can add little loops at the top of the bag so that you can clip a long strap onto your bag. Fold a piece of ribbon in half to make a loop and position it next to the strap, with the loop pointing downward and ⅜in (1cm) poking out above from the raw edge of the top of the lining. Pin it in place. Position the second loop on the other side, diagonally across from the first and next to the strap. To secure the straps, tab, and loops, start anywhere and sew around the top of the lining bag, using the right-hand side of the sewing-machine foot as your guide on the raw edge. Make sure the edges of the straps, tab, and loops stay at right angles to the edge of the lining as you sew, otherwise your straps may be wonky.

**14** With the faux fur bag inside out, insert the lining (with its right side out) inside the faux fur bag so their right sides are touching. Match up the side seams and all the top raw edges. Tuck the handles and tab down between the layers so that they don't get caught in the seam. Fabric-clip or pin all the way around the top. Starting at a seam, sew all the way around the top edge on the lining side, overlapping your stitches by ⅜in (1cm) when you come round to the beginning (see step 14 on page 95 of the Laptop Bag project). Tuck any tufts of fur inside as you go along.

**15** Turn the bag through to the right side by pulling the fabric out through the turning gap. Check that the straps, tab, and loops have successfully been sewn into the seam and push out all the corners.

**16** Sew up the turning gap (see page 122). Push the lining inside the bag and give the top edge a press if you can, but be careful not to have your iron too hot for the faux fur fabric. This fun fur bag is as functional for all your belongings as it is snuggly!

*Tips* Velvet is a tricky fabric to sew because it shifts as you stitch and frays easily, so I've just used it for the handles.

Use a stable cotton/linen fabric such as a quilting weight cotton, denim, or canvas for the main fabric. You are stablilizing it with fusible fleece so it doesn't have to be too sturdy. Choose a lighter weight cotton for the lining.

TO MAKE A SIMPLIFIED VERSION OF THE COSMETICS BAG:

Make a patch pocket (see page 123), instead of a zippered internal pocket. Use the same fabric dimensions, but cut it in two along the fold line and sew the pocket onto the right side of the lining.

Use fusible interfacing instead of fusible fleece. This will cut down on any bulky layers and make it easier to sew.

If you won't be using the bag with a long strap, leave out the strap tabs. This will also reduce the number of layers to sew through.

Omit the binding for the internal seams, and just neaten them by zigzag stitching close to the straight stitch and then trimming the seam neatly (see page 119).

# Cosmetics Bag

A roomy bag is always a must when traveling, and this one also has an internal zippered pocket and a wide base so it stands up. It can also be used with a long shoulder strap—why not make the strap on page 64 in a complementary fabric.

## YOU WILL NEED

Main fabric, 23⅝ x 27½in (60 x 70cm)—choose a fabric without a directional print (see page 113)

Lining fabric, 27½ x 27½in (70 x 70cm)

For contrast velvet handles: velvet fabric, 6¼ x 10¼in (16 x 26cm)

Fusible fleece, 23⅝ x 27½in (60 x 70cm)

16n (40cm) nylon zipper for main bag

8in (20cm) nylon zipper for letterbox pocket

Matching sewing thread

Basic sewing kit (see page 5)

Pressing ham

## FINISHED MEASUREMENTS

7½ x 9½ x 4in (19 x 24 x 10cm)

## TEMPLATES REQUIRED
## (SEE PAGE 132)

Main body
Letterbox zippered pocket

## CUTTING GUIDE

Cut 1 on fold in each of the main fabric, lining fabric, and fusible fleece:
Main body template

Cut 1 in the lining fabric:
Letterbox zippered pocket template

Cut 2 in the lining fabric:
Inner seam binding: 1⅝ x 23⅝in (4 x 60cm)

Cut 2 in each of the main fabric, lining fabric, and fusible fleece:
Zipper band: 2¾ x 13¼in (7 x 33.5cm)

Cut 2 in each of the main fabric (or velvet fabric, if using and make sure the direction/nap of the velvet runs along the length) and fusible fleece (omit the fusible fleece if you are using velvet as it will make the velvet too bulky):
Handle: 3⅛ x 10¼in (8 x 26cm)

Cut 2 in the main fabric (optional—see tip opposite):
Tab: 2⅜ x 2⅜in (6 x 6cm)

## LEARN HOW TO

- Insert an internal pocket with a letterbox zipper opening
- Make tube straps
- Make binding and use it to finish a raw edge
- Sew around curves
- Hand-baste (tack) binding in place

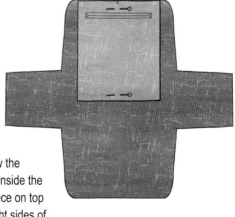

**1** Iron the fusible fleece pieces onto the wrong sides of the main fabric body, the main fabric zipper bands, and the main fabric handles.

**2** Transfer the template markings onto the right side of the main body piece and internal pocket with pen dots (see page 113). Fold the zipper bands in half along the long sides and mark their central points.

**3** On the wrong side of the pocket piece, follow step 1 on page 130 to mark out the letterbox position as a thin rectangle measuring ⅜ x 6¼in (1 x 16cm) as per the template. Also draw the central line and "V" shapes at either end inside the rectangle. Position the internal pocket piece on top of the lining main body piece, with the right sides of the fabrics together. Match up their central notches, making sure the top of the pocket is level with the top of the bag, and pin it in place.

**4** Follow steps 2–6 on pages 130–131 to sew the zippered internal pocket, with the 8in (20cm) zipper.

**5** Lay the 16in (40cm) zipper, right side down, on the right side of the long edge of one of the main zipper bands. Sew along the top edge, about ³⁄₁₆in (0.5cm) away from the zipper teeth, using a zipper foot on your machine (see page 130). Reverse stitch at the start and finish (see page 115). As you are sewing close to the zipper, you may need to get the zipper pull out the way (see step 5 on page 131).

**6** Lay the lining zipper band face down on the zipper so the right side of the lining fabric is touching the wrong side of the zipper. Pin it in place at right angles to the raw edge so that the pins stick out and can be seen.

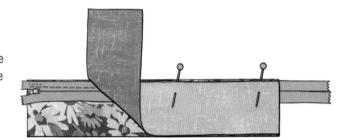

**7** Turn the piece over, and sew over the top of your first line of stitches, moving the zipper pull out of the way if necessary. Press (see page 117) both zipper bands away from the zipper teeth and pin them in place.

**8** Follow steps 5–7 to sew the second zipper band main and lining pieces to the other side of the zipper and then press and pin them away from the zipper teeth.

**9** Give the zipper bands another press on both sides. Cut away the excess part of the zipper. To keep the fabric away from the zipper teeth, topstitch (see page 114) ³⁄₁₆–³⁄₈in (0.5–1cm) away from the zipper teeth on each side of the zipper.

**10** Take the strap tab pieces of fabric and follow steps 1–2 on page 129 (for making a folded strap) with each piece.

**11** Fold one of the tabs in half, with its raw ends together, and position the raw ends on the center and on the right side of one end of the zipper band. Sew across the zipper band close to the edge to fix the tab in place, but go carefully as there are many layers to sew through including the zipper teeth. Repeat this step to sew the second tab to the other end of the zipper band.

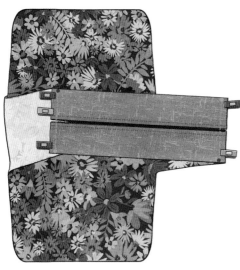

**12** Place the main-fabric body of the bag on the table with the right side facing you. Pin one short end of the zipper band to the edge of one of the main body's side flaps, with the right sides of the main fabrics together. Repeat to pin the other short end of the zipper band to the edge of the other side flap. Sew down each edge. Be careful as you sew through the zipper and strap tabs, and reverse stitch at each start and finish.

**13** Lay the main body lining piece on top of the main body piece. Line up the edge of one of the main body lining's side flaps with one side of the zipper band. The right side of the main body lining should be touching the lining side of the zipper band. Pin and then sew down this edge, through all the fabrics. As a guide, you can sew over the top of your first row of stitches on the side with the fleece, but you may need to stop to remove the fluff if it gets stuck over your machine's foot.

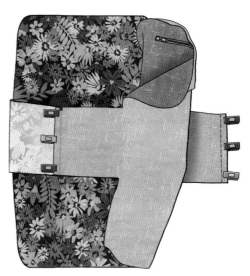

**14** Repeat step 13 to sew the edge of the lining's other flap to the other end of the zipper band. Trim both seams and grade them (see page 119).

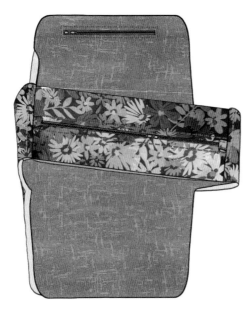

**15** Turn the piece "inside out" so the main body and lining have their wrong sides touching. Press the seams at either side of the zipper band away from the zipper band. I used a pressing ham to help me do this (see page 117). Topstitch across the top of each side flap of the main body, close to the seam. If the fabrics are too thick to sew through, you can leave the topstitching out.

**16** Take one of the pieces of fabric for the handle and follow steps 1–3 on page 128 to make a tube strap. Repeat for the second handle piece.

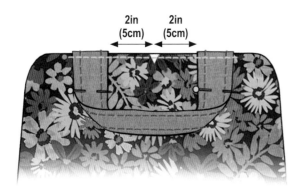

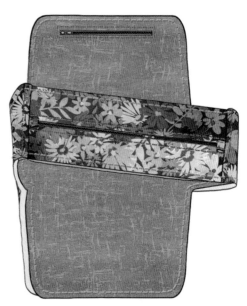

**17** Position one of the straps on the main-fabric side of the main bag, with their raw edges level and the inner sides of the strap 2in (5cm) away from the central notch on the main bag. Sew the strap in place near the edge. Placing a few pins in the strap will help it stay straight when you sew the bag together in the next steps. Repeat with the other strap on the opposite side.

**18** To keep all the layers in place, sew all the way around one side of the bag, about ³⁄₁₆in (0.5cm) from the edge, pivoting at the corners (see page 116). Then sew all the way around the other side. Trim the seams to even them up if necessary.

**19** Turn the bag "inside out" so the lining is on the outside. Match up the central notches on the zipper band with the center notches on the front and back of the bag. Start by pinning or fabric-clipping the bag together from the top where the handles are and then continue pinning or fabric-clipping down to the corners. Make sure all the layers are flat without any tucks, especially on the right side. Use fabric clips if the layers are thick. On the zipper band side, sew from one corner to the other on one side of the bag. Go carefully over the layers of the zipper band seams, straps, and around the curves. Reverse stitch at the start and finish. When you've finished, check that from the right side all the layers have been caught in the seam and there aren't any tucks. A few tucks may occur here and there because you have sewn from the lining side. You can easily unpick any minor mistakes (see page 117) and re-sew them. Repeat to sew the other side of the bag.

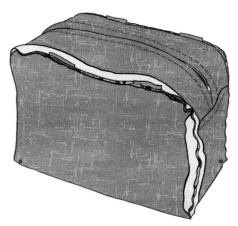

**20** Prepare the optional inner seam binding by pressing each piece as you would a folded strap (see steps 1–2 on page 129 for how to press it, but do not topstitch each side in step 2). Fold over the end of one piece of the binding by ⅜in (1cm) to the wrong side and place it on one of the corners of the bag with the right sides of the fabrics together. Secure it with a pin. Pin the rest of the binding in place with the pins sticking out at right angles from the seam, or use fabric clips. When you get to a curve, make a small snip in the binding at right angles to the edge so it can sit neatly around the curve. Start sewing the binding in place using the pressed-in crease on the binding as your guide for your stitching. As you come to the end, trim the binding off, leaving enough so you can fold ⅜in (1cm) to the wrong side and the binding can neatly cover the end of the seam. Pin in place and then continue sewing to the end and reverse stitch. Repeat with the second strip of binding on the other side of the bag.

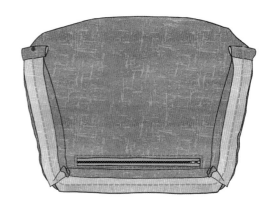

**21** Trim the seams on each side of the bag. Fold the binding over to enclose the raw edges. The free edge of the binding needs to just cover your first row of stitches by about ⅛in (a few millimetres). Hand-baste (tack) (see page 125) or fabric-clip the binding in place. At this point you can either machine sew through all thicknesses to fix the binding in place or slip stitch it in place all the way around by hand. Sometimes it's a bit difficult to get your machine stitching neat enough so to feel more in control, use slip stitches (see page 125). You're ready to head off on your holidays! Or even if you're not just now, you'll have a lovely bag that can carry everything you could possibly need on your travels.

*Tip* The slipstitches are small so they should almost disappear when you pull them up. You can slip stitch the hem on a skirt in place in the same way, which is known as "blind hemming." The stitches are almost invisible if the thread is a good match for the fabric.

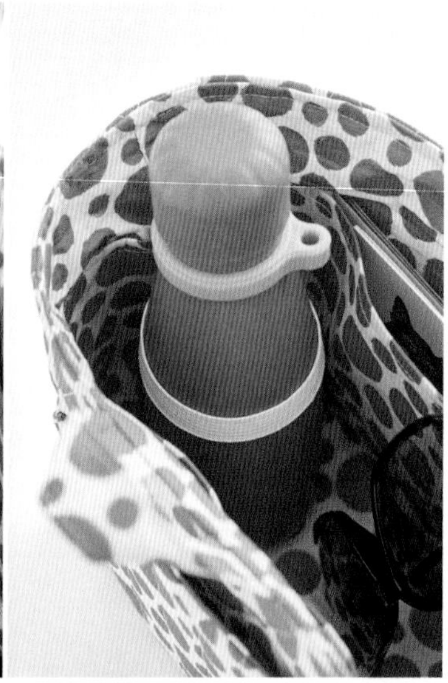

Skill level ✱✱✱

**Do you ever find yourself emptying your bag of its entire contents to find just one thing? This bag organizer with its numerous pockets and compartments can fit snugly into another bag to keep everything intact and easy to find.**

# Bag Organizer

### YOU WILL NEED

**For the outside:** Fabric, 14⅛ x 18⅞in (36 x 48cm)
Fusible fleece, 14¼ x 18¼in (36 x 48cm)

**For the lining:** Fabric, 14⅛ x 18⅞in (36 x 48cm) (you can use the same fabric as the outside as I have)
Iron-on interfacing, 14¼ x 18¼in (36 x 48cm)

**For the inner pocket:** Fabric, 14⅛ x 16⅛in (36 x 41cm)
Iron-on interfacing, 14⅛ x 16⅛in (36 x 41cm)

**For the straps:** Fabric, 2¾ x 14⅛in (7 x 36cm)
Iron-on interfacing, 2¾ x 14⅛in (7 x 36cm)

**For the outside patch pocket:** 2 pieces of fabric, each 5½ x 7⅛in (14 x 18cm)
Fusible fleece, 5½ x 7⅛in (14 x 18cm)

7⅞in (20cm) piece of ⅜in (1cm) wide elastic
1in (2.5cm) wide D-ring
Matching sewing thread
Basic sewing kit (see page 5)
Zipper foot

### FINISHED MEASUREMENTS

7½ x 9 x 4in (19 x 23 x 10cm)

### LEARN HOW TO

- Quilt with a quilting guide
- Create boxed corners
- Make tube straps
- Leaving a turning gap

*Tips* You don't have to use the same fabric for the outside, lining, and pockets. Use up what you have in your stash!

This organizer bag will fit into a bag with a base at least 9⅞in (25cm) long and 4¾in (12cm) wide. You can easily adjust the dimensions of your organizer bag by changing the base line measurement of your boxed corner in step 11.

You can choose to omit the quilting and, depending on how rigid your fabric is, you may not need to use interfacing or fusible fleece.

**1** Following the manufacturer's instructions, iron the fusible fleece onto the back of the fabric for the outside. Using a chalk marker and a ruler, draw two lines on the right side of the fabric from corner to corner to make a cross. Topstitch (see page 114) along these lines and use a quilting guide bar to sew the other parallel lines, all 1⅛in (3cm) apart (see steps 1–2 on page 15 in the Zippered Pillow Project). Quilting may make the rectangle shrink a little, so after quilting ensure that the lining piece is the same size and trim it to match if necessary.

**2** Iron the fusible fleece onto the back of one of the patch pocket pieces. You can either use a ruler and chalk marker to draw vertical parallel lines ¾in (2cm) away from each other and then topstitch along the lines, or use your quilting guide bar to topstitch the lines across the pocket piece (see page 127).

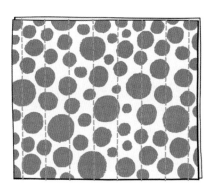

**3** Place the two patch pocket pieces together with the right sides touching and sew around the edge, leaving a 2¾in (7cm) turning gap in the long bottom edge (see page 122). Reverse stitch at the start and finish (see page 115). Cut off the corners (see page 119) and then turn the pocket through to the right side by pulling the fabric out through the turning gap.

**4** Iron the interfacing onto the wrong side of the strap piece. Fold it in half along its length with right sides together and sew down the long side. Use a safety pin to turn the strap to the right side, and then press it and topstitch down each long side (see steps 1–3 on page 128).

**5** Cut 2in (5cm) off one end of the strap, fold it in half around the D-ring, and fabric-clip in place. Cut the remaining part of the strap in half.

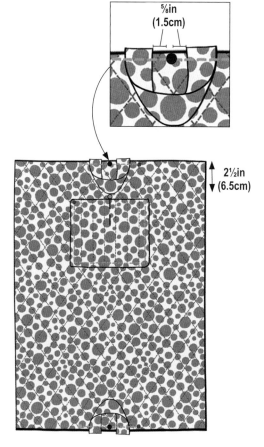

**6** Fold the quilted main bag piece in half along its width to find the center of each short end. Mark these points with pen dots. Fold the pocket in half along one of its long sides and mark the center with a pin. Align the center of the patch pocket with one of the pen dots on the main bag piece, and position the pocket on the right side of the main bag piece, 2½in (6.5cm) down from the top raw edge, with its turning gap at the bottom. Pin the pocket in place and topstitch along the short sides and lower edge using the right-hand side of the sewing-machine foot as your guide on the edge of the pocket. Reverse stitch at the start and finish. Using the central pen dots on the main bag piece, position the ends of one of the long strap pieces ⅝in (1.5cm) either side of the center. Fabric-clip the strap in place so the raw edges line up with the raw edge of the main bag. Fabric-clip the other strap in place at the other end of the main bag piece in the same way. Sew across the straps to keep them in place using the right-hand side of your sewing-machine foot as your guide on the edge of the fabric.

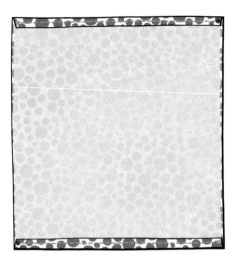

**7** Iron the interfacing onto the wrong side of the inner pocket piece. Make a double hem (see page 121) along the two short edges of the inner pocket piece. Topstitch the hems in place along the middle of each hem and press (see page 117).

**8** Fold the inner pocket piece in half with the finished hems together and press the fold. Unfold and lay out flat, with the right side facing upward. Use the measurements on the illustration to draw out the compartment lines using a ruler and a chalk or non-permanent marker.

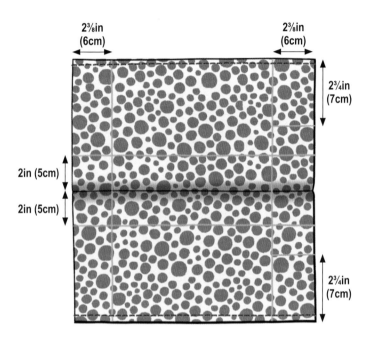

2⅜in (6cm)

2⅜in (6cm)

2¾in (7cm)

2in (5cm)

2in (5cm)

2¾in (7cm)

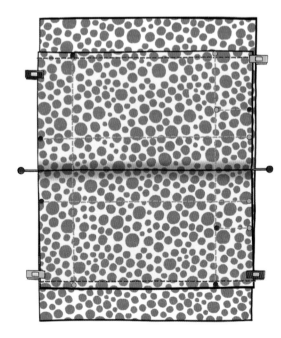

**9** Iron the interfacing for the lining onto the back of the lining piece. Fold the lining in half with its short sides together and mark the center on each edge with a pin at right angles. Lay the inner pocket on top of the lining so the wrong side of the inner pocket is touching the right side of the lining. Make sure the inner pocket sits in the center of the lining by matching up the crease in the pocket with the pins in the lining and pin or fabric-clip it in place. Topstitch down all the drawn lines, through all the layers, reverse stitching at the start and finish of each line.

**10** With the right sides together, fold the lining piece in half and fabric-clip it in place down the raw edges. Check that the tops of the inner pockets line up within the seams. Fold the elastic in half to make a loop. From the inside of the lining piece on the left-hand side, push the raw edges of the elastic between the two layers of the pocket so it is sandwiched between them with ⅜in (1cm) poking out. Do the same with the fabric tab that has the D-ring, making it flush with the right-hand-side raw edge. Both the elastic and tab should be positioned 3⅛in (8cm) down from the top raw edge. To allow you to sew down the tab side, you will need to change to a zipper foot (see page 130) so you can keep to the ⅜in (1cm) seam allowance. On the other side with the elastic, you can use your general-purpose foot. Once sewn, finger press a crease along the bottom fold.

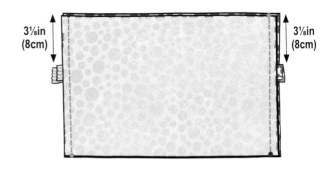

3⅛in (8cm)  3⅛in (8cm)

**11** To make the boxed corners (see steps 1–2 on page 128), push out one of the corners of the lining bag from the inside with your finger and then flatten out the pointed end. Push a pin through the seam to match it up with the crease on the other side (see page 120). Draw a line across the corner to make a triangle shape with a 4in (10cm) base line. Sew across this base line with reverse stitch at the start and finish and then trim off the end of the triangle. Repeat for the other corner.

**12** Take the outside bag piece and fold it in half with right sides touching, matching up the two short sides. Sew down the two sides with reverse stitching at the start and finish, in the same way as you did in step 10 (except without the D-ring and elastic). Make boxed corners on the outer piece, in the same way as you did in step 11.

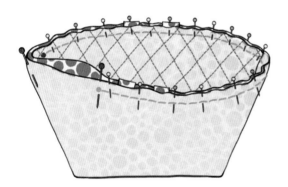

**13** Turn the outside bag right side out but keep the lining bag with its wrong side out. Place the outside bag into the lining bag. Match up the two side seams with a pin and pin the bags together all the way around the top, leaving a turning gap in between one of the side seams and one side of a strap. This will ensure that both straps are machine-sewn securely in place. Sew the bags together around the top edge on the fleece side and reverse stitch at the start and finish. Trim the seam to neaten it.

**14** Turn the bag through to the right side through the turning gap. Press the top edge, making sure the lining doesn't show above the outer bag. If you have difficulty keeping the lining down and not showing above the outer fabric, you can hand-baste (tack) it in place (see page 125) before you topstitch all the way around the top edge. Use the right-hand side of your sewing-machine foot on the top edge of the bag as your guide. When you get round to the beginning, overlap your stitches by ⅜in (1cm) (see page 115). Unpick any hand stitches and press the top edge well. Now you can ditch that bottomless pit and keep everything to hand in each bag you use, whether it's a tote bag for days out or a briefcase for work.

*Tip* To create a zero-waste version: If you cut out an inner pocket measuring 14⅛ x 18⅞in (36 x 48cm)—instead of 14⅛ x 16⅛in (36 x 41cm)—you can trim off 2¾in (7cm) from a short side to make the correct strap size of 2¾ x 14⅛in (7 x 36cm). The remaining piece will be the correct inner pocket size—14⅛ x 16⅛in (36 x 41cm), so it's zero waste! Do the same with the iron-on interfacing.

Skill level ✳✳✳

Don't cramp your style with a dull black workbag—instead keep your laptop snug and protected in this practical and stylish design.

# Laptop Bag

## YOU WILL NEED

**For the main bag:** Fabric, 17¾ x 26⅜in (45 x 67cm) (I used polyester bouclé)

**For the lining:** Fabric, 17¾ x 26⅜in (45 x 67cm) (I used polar fleece)

**For the inner pocket:** 2 pieces of cotton canvas, each 8¼ x 11¾in (21 x 30cm)

**For the inner side tabs:** cotton canvas, 1⅝ x 4in (4 x 10cm)

**For the inner straps:** 2 pieces of cotton canvas, each 3½ x 10¼in (9 x 26cm)

**For the lining and main bag:** 2 pieces of iron-on interfacing, each 17¾ x 26⅜in (45 x 67cm)

Matching sewing thread

2 x 5⅞in- (15cm-)long pieces of ¾in (2cm)-wide hook-and-loop tape

86⅝in (220cm)-long piece of 1³⁄₁₆–1⅝in- (3–4cm-)wide cotton webbing

Magnetic clasp

Basic sewing kit (see page 5)

Quilter's tape/sticky tape

## FINISHED MEASUREMENTS

12½ x 16in (32 x 41cm)

## TEMPLATE REQUIRED (SEE PAGE 134)

Curved Top

## LEARN HOW TO

- Make tube straps
- Sew on a hook-and-loop fastening
- Attach a magnetic clasp
- Sew wrap-around webbing straps

*Tip* If your fabric is a bit stretchy (like fleece) it may be easier to cut out the bag shape in iron-on interfacing first. Then iron the interfacing onto the wrong side of your fabric (check that the grainline is correct—see page 112). Use the interfacing piece as a template to cut out your fabric.

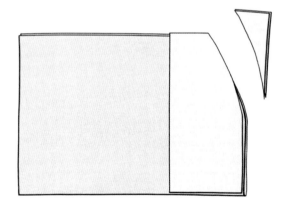

**1** Draft and cut out a paper rectangle measuring 17¾ x 13³⁄₁₆in (45 x 33.5cm), and fold it in half along its length. Place the template so that its curved edge is on one of the non-folded corners, draw around the curve, and then cut along the curve through both layers of paper.

**2** Open out the paper rectangle. Fold the main fabric, lining fabric, and interfacing pieces in half, matching their short sides together. Pin the straight long edge of the paper template on the fold of the lining piece and cut along the curves. Repeat for the main and interfacing pieces. Iron the interfacing pieces onto the wrong side of the main and lining pieces.

**3** Place the inner pocket pieces together with their right sides facing. Sew all the way around, leaving a 4in (10cm) gap in one of the long sides. Turn the pocket through to the right side and press (see page 117). Topstitch (see page 114) along the top edge (the opposite edge to the turning gap) (see steps 1–3 on page 123).

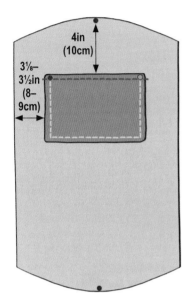

**4** To find the center of the fleece lining piece, fold it in half, matching the long sides together. Mark the center of each curved end with a dot. On the right side of the lining piece, position the pocket 4in (10cm) from the top and 3⅛–3½in (8–9cm) from each side. Pin the pocket in place and topstitch it along the sides and lower edge, using the right-hand side of the sewing-machine foot as your guide on the edge of the pocket (see page 118). Reverse stitch at the start and finish (see page 115).

**5** Take one of the inner strap pieces. Fold one of its short ends to the wrong side by ⅜in (1cm). Then fold it in half along its length with the right side of the fabric together. Sew down the long raw edge, reverse stitching at the start and finish and sewing over the fold right to the end (see page 129). Repeat with the other strap.

**6** Use a safety pin to turn the strap through to the right side (see page 128). Topstitch down each long edge and along the short folded end using the right-hand side of the sewing-machine foot as your guide on the edge of the strap.

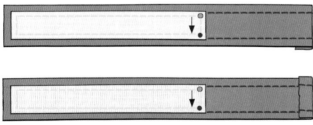

**7** Fold the raw end of one of the straps over by ⅜in (1cm) and press. Repeat for the second strap. Place the straps on the table so that one of the straps has its raw end facing upward and the other with its raw end facing downward. Pull the hook-and-loop tape strip apart and position one piece on each of the straps, ⅜in (1cm) away from the sewn end. You can use quilter's tape or sticky tape here to keep the hook-and-loop tape in place. Using an off-white spool thread to match the hook-and-loop tape and a bobbin thread to match your strap fabric, start sewing at a short end and sew all the way around the tape as near to the edge of the tape as you can, overlapping your stitches by ⅜in (1cm) when you get round to the beginning.

**8** Place the lining piece on the table with the pocket at the top. Using the central dot, position the raw edge of one strap in the center, 2⅜in (6cm) up from the bottom curved edge. Position the raw edge of the other strap in the center, 13in (33cm) away from the top curved edge. Use quilter's tape or sticky tape to keep the straps in place. Sew across each strap ⅜in (1cm) away from the raw edge and along the creases made in step 7. Reverse stitch at the start and finish.

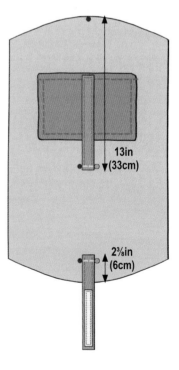

**9** On the lining piece, flip one of the straps back on itself and pin it in place (if it's too thick, use sticky tape to keep it in place). Repeat with the other strap. At this point, check that your laptop will fit underneath the straps when the straps are stuck together. Sew across the folded ends of the straps, through all thicknesses and ⅜in (1cm) from each fold, reverse stitching at each start and finish (see the illustration below).

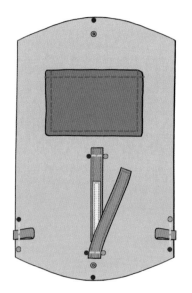

**10** Take the piece of fabric for the inner side tabs and follow steps 1–2 on page 129 to make a folded strap. Topstitch down each side, close to the edge. Cut the strap in half. Fold each piece in half and press. Position the tabs on the right side of the fleece lining, ¾in (2cm) from the curved end as shown, with their loops facing inward. Sew them in place close to the edge, within the seam allowance. Fix the socket part of the magnetic clasp on the lower edge, 1³⁄₁₆in (3cm) up from the central dot (see page 131). Fix the ball part of the magnetic clasp on the upper edge, 1³⁄₁₆in (3cm) down from the central dot.

**11** Take the piece of fabric for the outer bag. To start positioning the webbing, place a raw end 16½in (42cm) from the bottom curved edge and 4in (10cm) in from the right-hand side. To keep the strap in place, use quilter's tape to stick it down on the underside or sticky tape to hold in place on the right side and use fabric clips at the top and bottom edges. Continue sticking the strap in place around the outer bag piece, making the handles 13in (33cm) in length from edge to edge. Ensure the straps lie parallel to each other on the bag piece. When you come back to the start, trim the strap if necessary so that it overlaps the raw end of the other strap by ¾in (2cm). Then tuck the edge you have just trimmed under by ⅜in (1cm), place it on top of the other strap's raw end, and fabric-clip in place. Using the right-hand side of the sewing-machine foot as your guide on the edge of the webbing, start sewing at the overlap and topstitch all the way around one side of the strap, so you sew along both sides of the webbing. Pivot (see page 116) when you get 1½in (4cm) away from the curved edge of the bag (you can mark this point with a chalk line across the strap to help you), sew across the handle, pivot again and then carry on sewing down the opposite side. When you come round to the beginning, sew over the join and just past it, and reverse stitch for about ¾in (a few centimeters). Sew around the other side of the strap in the same way.

1½in (4cm)

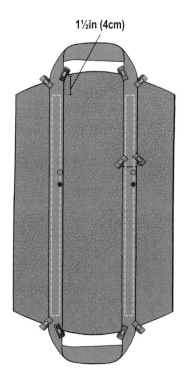

**12** Fold the main bag piece in half with the right sides together, matching up the curved edges, then pin and sew down the sides. Reverse stitch at each start and finish. Cut off the corners (see page 119).

**13** Fold the lining in half with the right sides together and match up the curved edges. Pin and sew down the two short sides, leaving a turning gap of 6in (15cm) in one side. Reverse stitch at each start and finish. Cut off the corners.

**14** Turn the main bag right side out and insert it into the lining bag so that the right sides are touching. Match up the raw edges. Pin the pieces together at right angles to the top edge, or fabric clip all the way around the top edge. Match up each side seam of the lining to each side seam on the main bag using a pin (see page 120). Starting along a side, sew around the top. Keep in mind that the top edge is curved and you will need to stop on the side seam, with your needle down to pivot and change direction to create a side 'V' shape to your bag. Sew on the main bag side. Overlap your stitches by ⅜in (1cm) when you get back to the beginning. Grade the seam (see page 119).

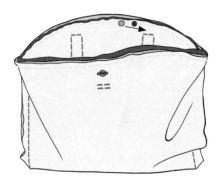

**15** Turn the bag through to the right side by pulling and pushing the fabric out through the turning gap in the lining.

**16** Tuck in the raw edges of the turning gap and pin or fabric-clip them in place. Sew along the turning gap using the right-hand side of the sewing-machine foot as your guide on the edge of the fabric. Reverse stitch at the start and finish. Push the lining inside the main bag. You can choose to topstitch around the top of the bag if the lining won't stay down in place, but if the layers are too thick you can leave out the topstitching. Bags for work don't have to be dull, so brighten things up with a colorful one! It might just improve your work day!

*Tips* You can use this bag to carry anything that needs to stay flat, such as documents or artwork.

The case has inner tabs so that you can attach a shoulder strap (see page 64).

# Chapter 3

## *Garments*

This simple apron provides great coverage for when you're busy baking, sewing, or gardening. The cross-back design means that you can easily slip it over your head without the need for any awkward ties.

# Cross-back Apron

## YOU WILL NEED

Main fabric, 2½yd of 145-in wide (2.2m of 115cm-wide) (I used linen)

Matching sewing thread

Basic sewing kit (see page 5)

Compass or dinner plate with a diameter of at least 9¾in (25cm)

## FINISHED MEASUREMENTS

Length from top of neckline to bottom edge: 33in (84cm)

Width: 52⅜in (133cm)

## TEMPLATES REQUIRED (SEE PAGES 142–143)

Front

Back

Facing

Pocket

## LEARN HOW TO

■ Draft up a paper pattern

■ Sew French seams

■ Create a patch pocket

■ Sew a facing

**1** Following the instructions on page 143, scale up the back and front template pieces. Cut out the paper template pieces.

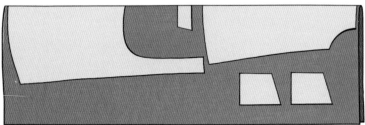

*Tips* If the template for the back piece on page 143 is too big to fit onto your fabric, you can cut it in two along line C. Remember to add a ⅜in (1cm) seam allowance to both edges, then cut out the two pieces from the fabric and sew them together. You could French seam (see page 120) these two pieces together for a neater finish if your fabric isn't too thick.

The apron dimensions are for one size, but the straps can be easily made longer or shorter. You could also shorten the apron along the bottom edges of the front and back pieces.

**2** Fold your fabric in half so the selvages (see page 112) are together. Place the front, back, and facing template pieces on the fold as per the layout diagram. Pin the templates in place and then cut out the pieces from the fabric. Only the front and facing need to be cut out on the fold, but to make sure the grainline is correct you can place the back pattern piece on the fold too, as shown, and then cut the back fabric piece in half along the fold.

**3** Lay the front and back pieces on the table with the wrong sides of the fabrics facing upward. Flip one back piece onto the front piece with the wrong sides together. Match up the straight sides and pin together. Sew these pieces together using a French seam (see page 120). Repeat to sew the second back piece to the other side of the front piece using a French seam.

**4** Press the seams (see page 117) toward the back of the apron and then topstitch them (see page 114) in place on the right side of the apron, as close to the seam as you can (about ⅛in/ 4mm away).

**5** Follow steps 1–2 on page 123 to make the two patch pockets. In step 1, leave a 4in (10cm) turning gap at the bottom of each pocket.

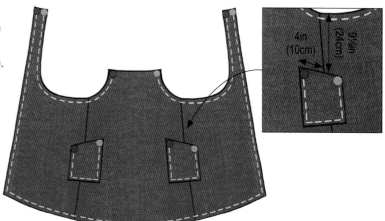

**6** Next, you will make a double hem (see page 121) all around the apron's raw edges except along the top of the straps and the top neck edge. To do this, press these edges to the wrong side of the fabric by about ¼in (7mm). Press these folded edges to the wrong side of the fabric again by about ¼in (7mm), so that you can't see any raw edges. It's better to keep the hem as narrow as you can, otherwise it will be difficult to sew around the curves. Pin the hems in place and topstitch them on the right side of the apron in the middle of the double hem and about ⅛in (4mm) away from the edge. If the hems are thick, go slowly and pull the fabric through from behind the sewing-machine foot as it feeds through, to maintain the stitch length. Position the pockets over each side seam of the apron, 9½in (24cm) down from the armhole, and 4in (10cm) onto the front. If you prefer, you can position the pockets closer to each other, so that they are just on the front section of the apron. Pin the pockets in place and see how they feel for comfort. Make sure that both pockets are pinned symmetrically, then topstitch around the two sides and bottom edges, using the right-hand side of the sewing-machine foot as your guide on the edge of the pocket (see page 118). Reverse stitch at the start and finish (see page 115).

**7** Lay the apron on the table with the right side facing down. Cross the straps so that the strap on the left-hand side goes to the right-hand side of the top of the apron, and the strap on the right-hand side goes to the left-hand side of the top of the apron. Match up the raw short edges of the straps with the raw straight edge of the top of the apron. Sew across the top of the apron to fix the straps in place, using the right-hand side of the sewing-machine foot as your guide on the edge of the fabric. The straps come out at the top at a slight angle.

**8** To prepare the facing, fold the longest side to the wrong side of the fabric by ⅝in (1.5cm) and press. Do the same to fold the two short sides to the wrong side of the fabric by ⅝in (1.5cm) and press.

**9** To make neat, mitred corners, open out the pressed corners and then fold a triangle in from each corner (see page 121). Re-fold the sides over the top of the triangles on the facing and press, to create neat corners.

**10** Lay the right side of the facing onto the right side of the straps. Match up the raw edges. Using a ⅜in (1cm) seam allowance, sew along the top edge of the apron, making sure that the facing is still folded over at its short edges so that they don't extend beyond the apron.

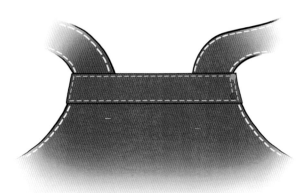

**11** Turn the apron over so that the right side is facing upward. Flip the facing over to the right side of the apron. Give the facing a press, adjusting it and tucking the sides under if necessary to make the facing fit with the sides of the apron. Make sure the straps and the sides of the apron are out of the way. Sew all the way around the facing, using the right-hand side of the sewing-machine foot as your guide on the edge of the facing. Overlap your stitches when you get back to where you started (see page 115). Your apron is finished—now you can look for that special recipe or sewing project and stay spotless while getting creative!

Skill level ✳✳

This simple shape makes the perfect easy-to-wear cover-up. Choose a floaty, lightweight fabric such as satin, viscose, or cotton lawn. You could slip this jacket over a tee and jeans for the best laid-back vibe, or use it to elevate an outfit with some extra glamour.

# Duster Jacket

## YOU WILL NEED

**For the front:** 2 pieces of fabric, each 13¾ x 30¼in (35 x 77cm)

**For the back:** fabric, 29⅛ x 30¼in (74 x 77cm)

**For the sleeves:** 2 pieces of fabric, each 10⅝ x 25⅝in (27 x 65cm)

Matching sewing thread

Basic sewing kit (see page 5)—use a sewing-machine needle size 70/10 for lightweight fabrics

Spray starch (optional)

## FINISHED MEASUREMENTS

Length from back of neck to hem: 28¼in (72cm)

## TEMPLATES REQUIRED (SEE PAGE 137)

Front diagram

Back diagram

Back Neck template

Sleeve diagram

## CUTTING GUIDE

Cut 2 of each of the following in the front and sleeve fabrics:

Front

Sleeve

Fold the fabric rectangle for the back in half, matching up the long sides so it measures 14½ x 30¼in (37 x 77cm), cut 1 of the following on the fold, then cut the Back Neck template out of the Back piece (see page 137):

Back

## LEARN HOW TO

- Sew with lightweight fabrics
- Draft out a simple pattern
- Sew a long double hem
- Insert a sleeve using the "flat" method

*Tips* This pattern's simple shape makes it gender-neutral and versatile. By changing the length, you can create different styles from a dressing gown to a cropped jacket.

The size equates to a women's US size 12–14 (UK size 16–18) but the fit is generous. It can be scaled up or down as the pattern is based on simple rectangles. For a US size 8–10 (UK size 12–14), reduce the pattern by ¾in (2cm) around all the edges. For a US size 16–18 (UK size 20–22), add ¾in (2cm) around all the edges.

**1** With the right sides of the fabric together, lay the two front pieces on the back piece with the top (shoulder) edges matching. Pin and then sew across each of the shoulder edges, using a ⅝in (1.5cm) seam allowance (see tip below) and reverse stitching at each start and finish (see page 115). Reinforce the seam with a row of zigzag stitching (see page 119) close to the straight stitching, and then trim the seam. Alternatively, to prevent any fraying, you can sew French seams (see page 120).

**2** Transfer the notch from the sleeve template to each of the fabric sleeve pieces (see page 112). Open out the jacket along the shoulder seams so the right side of the fabric is facing you. Lay a sleeve piece right side down on the jacket, so the right sides of the fabrics are touching. Match the central notch on the sleeve to the shoulder seam of the jacket body. Pin in place, making sure

the shoulder seam lies toward the back of the jacket, and then sew down the edge, ⅝in (1.5cm) seam allowance. Reinforce the seam with zigzag stitch and trim to the zigzag. Repeat with the other sleeve on the opposite side. Alternatively, to prevent any fraying, you can sew French seams. Press each seam (see page 117) toward the sleeve.

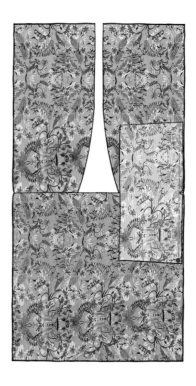

**3** With the right sides touching, fold the jacket so the raw edges of the side seams and underarm sleeve seams match up. Match up the underarm seams with a pin (see page 120). Pin and then sew from the end of the sleeve down toward the hem, with a ⅝in (1.5cm) seam allowance. When you sew the underarm corner, sew a few stitches just beyond the sleeve seam you stitched in the previous step, then pivot at the yellow dot (see page 116) and sew down the side to the bottom hem. Reverse stitch at the start and finish. Repeat on the other side so both sides are sewn in the same direction.

*Tips* Sewing with lightweight fabrics can be tricky as pins tend to slide out and fabric clips can be too heavy. If this is the case for your fabric, hand-baste (tack) the seam or hem in place (see page 125) before using the machine to prevent the fabric shifting.

To help you further, using spray starch (find it in the laundry aisle) is an excellent way of stiffening fabric, making floppy material easier to sew.

The seam allowances for this project are ⅝in (1.5cm) as they are for most dressmaking patterns. Use the ⅝in (1.5cm) guide on your machine's throatplate (see page 118).

**4** To prevent any fraying and reinforce the seams, zigzag stitch along all the seams you have sewn in the step 3, in between your stitching and the edge of the fabric, pivoting at the underarm. Use a smaller or longer zigzag if necessary to prevent any puckering. To reinforce the underarm seam further and help it lie flat, sew over your existing lines of straight stitching with another line of straight stitching, just in the underarm corner and a few centimetres up each side (see page 119). To ease any bunching in the underarm area, snip into the corner as close to the stitching as you can (see page 119).

**5** Next, you will press a double hem (see page 121) all around the two front edges, the bottom edge of the jacket, the neck edges, and the raw edges of the sleeves. To do this, fold each of these edges to the wrong side by ⅜in (1cm) and press, then fold them to the wrong side again by ⅜in (1cm) and press in place. You can spray starch these edges before you press the hems to make your pressing easier. The starch makes the fabric more rigid and the hem stay put so it will be easier to sew. At the bottom corner, press the hem of each front piece first, followed by the bottom hem. To make doubly sure the corner fold and the hem around the neck will stay in place as you sew, hand-baste (tack) the hems in place using long running stitches which can then be removed after machine sewing (see page 125).

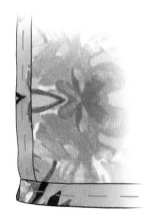

**6** Starting at a side seam, topstitch (see page 114) all around the front, neckline, and bottom edges of the jacket where you've pressed the double hem. Make sure your bobbin and spool thread match the fabric well. Sew on the right side of the fabric so that you can check your stitches are looking good as you go along. Use the right-hand side of the sewing-machine foot as your guide on the edge of the fabric (see page 118), and as you sew, pull the hem a little bit taut around the curve of the neckline to help it lie flat. When you get round to the beginning, overlap your stitches by ⅜in (1cm) (see page 115) and add a few reverse stitches for good measure. If you're using fabric clips remember to take them out in time so they don't cause crooked stitches. Take your time—there's a lot to sew!

**7** Sew the sleeve hem in the same way as for step 6, starting at the underarm seam and overlapping your stitches by ⅜in (1cm) when you come round to the beginning. Use the free arm of your machine to help you (see page 115).

*Tip* The open front and dropped shoulders create a relaxed look and you can easily adapt the pattern to add pockets (see page 123). You could also add a decorative hemline by sewing on a contrast bias-binding (see page 87) or a lace trim.

This easy and relaxed top requires just two body measurements to make it fit you perfectly, and because it's so simple you can really let loose with your choice of fabric! You can also mix up the design by leaving out the elastic in the hem.

# Tailor-made Top

## YOU WILL NEED

**For the top:** main fabric, 26⅜ x 51¼in (67 x 130cm) for a US size 12 (UK size 16) or use your own bespoke measurements (see step 2)

**For the neck facing:** main fabric, 15¾ x 15¾in (40 x 40cm)

**For the elasticated hem version:** ⅜in (1cm) wide elastic long enough to fit around your hips minus 2in (5cm)

Small button (with a shank), about ⅜in (1cm) in diameter

Matching sewing thread

Embroidery floss (thread)

Basic sewing kit (see page 5)

Safety pin

## FINISHED MEASUREMENTS

Custom size

## TEMPLATE REQUIRED (SEE PAGE 139)

Neck Facing

## CUTTING GUIDE

As with all dressmaking pattern layouts, you will need to cut out your fabric rectangle with the longest side (the body length—see step 2) parallel to the selvage (see page 112).

## LEARN HOW TO

- Take your measurements
- Draft out a pattern
- Sew a hem
- Insert a neck facing and understitch
- Create an elasticated hem

**1** First, you will need to take your hip and body length measurements. These will allow you to draft out the rectangular pattern piece for the top. Using a mirror will help you take the measurements accurately, and you may also need help from a friend. You will need two measurements: your hip circumference and body length.

**Please note:** First, measure around the fullest part of your bust. If your bust circumference measurement is more than your hip measurement, use your bust measurement for the rectangle's width.

**For the hip measurement:** With your feet together, wrap a flexible tape around your hips, measuring across the fullest part.

**For the body length:** Take the measurement from your shoulder to where you want your top to finish. If you're putting elastic in the bottom hem, you may like to add 2–4in (5–10cm) extra to allow for the top to blouson out.

**2** To work out the dimensions of the rectangle you need:

**For the rectangle's width:** Divide your hip measurement by 2 and add 4¾in (12cm) (for "ease," see tip on page 105).

**For the rectangle's length:** Multiply your body length measurement by 2 and add 2⅜in (6cm) for the hems.

For example: If your hip measurement were 43½in (110cm) (about a US size 12/UK size 16):
43½in (110cm) divided by 2 = 21¾ (55cm) + 4¾in (12cm) = 26½in (67cm).
The rectangle must measure 26½in (67cm) in width.

If your body length measurement were 24½in (62cm):
24½in (62cm) multiplied by 2 = 49in (124cm) + 2⅜in (6cm) = 51⅜in (130cm).
The rectangle must measure 51⅜in (130cm) in length.

**3** You can either draft out the measurements directly onto the fabric, or you can draft out a rectangular paper pattern, pin it to the fabric, and use it as a template to cut out the rectangle. Finish the long edges of your fabric rectangle with zigzag stitch (see page 114), using the right-hand side of your sewing-machine foot as a guide on the edge of the fabric (see page 118). Using the side of the foot will prevent you getting too close to the edge of the fabric where the stitches could pucker up the fabric. If the zigzag stitching won't lie flat because the fabric isn't sturdy enough, you can sew a straight stitch close to each raw edge instead or use spray starch to make it stiffer.

*Tips* In dressmaking, you need to allow for movement and comfort in your clothes. This added allowance is called "ease" and can change how a garment fits, either making it loose-fitting or cling to your body, for example. For this top, 4¾in (12cm) in total has been added to the width to give it a relaxed style and fit.

As this top is made out of one piece of fabric (with no shoulder seams), don't use a directional print (see page 113) because the fabric would appear upside down on one of the sides.

This top has a one-size neck opening which may not suit everyone. Make a mock-up with an old bedsheet or scrap fabric to check how it fits for you.

**4** If you are making the top with an elasticated hem, prepare the bottom hem by folding one of the short sides of the rectangle to the wrong side by ⅜in (1cm) and press (see page 117). Fold it to the wrong side again by ¾in (2cm) and press. Repeat with the other short side of the rectangle. If you are making a top without elastic in the hem, press each short side of the rectangle by ⅝in (1.5cm) to the wrong side and then by ⅝in (1.5cm) again.

Press well along here

Place a pin here

**5** Fold the rectangle in half along its length with the right sides of the fabric together. Then fold it in half again along its width, so that the fabric is folded into four layers. Press the folds, especially in the center where the folds meet. These pressed-in creases will mark the horizontal shoulder line and the vertical center line of the top. Put a pin through the center, open out the rectangle, and mark the center with a pen dot on the right side of the fabric.

**6** To make the neck facing paper pattern, trace the template pieces on page 139, cut them out, and join them together along the dotted line. Fold a piece of spare paper measuring 15¾ x 15¾in (40cm x 40cm) in half and place the template on the fold (see page 112). Draw around the template and then remove the template. With the piece of paper still folded, carefully cut around where you've drawn so that when you open it out you have the complete neck facing shape.

**7** Pin the neck facing template onto the wrong side of the 15¾ x 15¾in (40 x 40cm) square of fabric. Draw around all the edges. If you are using a dark-colored fabric, use a chalk marker or a pen. If you're using a light-colored fabric, a pencil will show up well. Use a ruler to extend the center lines and shoulder lines to find the very center, and mark this point with a pen dot on the wrong side of the fabric.

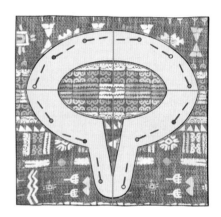

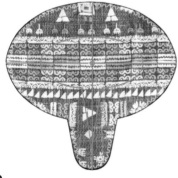

**8** Remove the paper pattern. Sew on the outside line of the neck facing, directly on top of the line you've drawn, using a zigzag (or a straight stitch, if your fabric is very lightweight). Trim around the outside of the neck facing, close to the zigzag stitching.

**9** Place the rectangle of fabric for the top on the table with the right side facing up. Place the neck facing down onto the center of the top, with the right sides of the fabrics touching. Line up the pressed creases on the top fabric with the horizontal and vertical lines on the neck facing. Use a pin to line up the central pen dots (see page 120). Pin the facing in place on the top. Using straight stitch, sew around the inner shape of the neck facing, directly on the drawn line. Pivot (see page 116) where there are corners and go steadily around the curves. Overlap your stitches by about ⅜in (1cm) when you get back to where you started (see page 115).

**10** To reinforce the point of the triangle, sew over the "V" of the point again (see page 119), stitching over your existing stitches and about ¾in (2cm) up each side from the bottom of the "V." Make sure you sew exactly over the top of your first line of stitching and that your pivot at the bottom is in the same place. For accuracy, stop sewing ⅜in (1cm) before the point and use the handwheel (see page 115) to do those final stitches to the point. Cut out the inner shape of the neck facing, about ³⁄₁₆in (0.5cm) away from your stitching. Trim the corners and cut into all the curves (see page 119). The more snips the better, but make sure you don't cut through your stitches. To make the "V" shape lie flat, snip down the point as far as you can go—even one millimeter can make a difference!

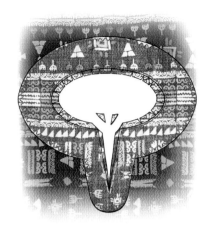

**11** To make the neck facing lie flat on the inside of the top, pin it near to the seam, through the facing on the right side and including the seam allowance underneath. Then sew about ⅛in (3mm) away from the seam on the facing side, sewing through the seam allowance at the same time (see page 123). This is called understitching and it's a really effective way of creating a flat neckline that prevents the facing rolling toward the outside. Sew as far as you can around the neck opening (don't stitch into the "V" shape), and reverse stitch at the start and finish (see page 115). Press the facing to the inside of the top.

**12** Fold the top in half with the right sides together so the hems meet. At one of the sides, place a pin 10in (25cm) down from the shoulder. Repeat with the other side. Try on the top, check that the armhole openings are right for you, and adjust if necessary. Open out the pressed hems and pin them together at the bottom edges. Sew down the side seam from the pin to the hem, using a ⅝in (1.5cm) seam allowance and reverse stitching at the start and finish. Repeat on the other side seam.

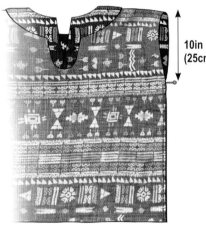

10in (25cm)

**13** Press the side seams open (see page 117) and then press a ⅝in (1.5cm) hem to the wrong side of the fabric all around the sleeve armhole. On the right side of the top, topstitch (see page 114) around the sleeve opening using a ⅜in (1cm) seam allowance. Start at the underarm first, doing a few stitches along the bottom of the sleeve opening over the seam. Then pivot and sew up one side and down the other, overlapping your stitches when you get to the beginning again. It's a tricky shape to sew, so take it slowly and keep moving the fabric out of the way as you sew so that you don't make any unwanted tucks.

**14** Pin the double hem in place (see page 121) around the bottom edge of the top, where you pressed it previously. You can try the top on now to check you like the hem position and change it if necessary.

**15** If you are making a top without an elasticated hem, topstitch the double hem in place, using the sewing machine's throat plate guide to sew with a ⅜in (1cm) seam allowance from the bottom edge of the top (see page 118). You can sew on the right or wrong side of the fabric, but check that the bobbin thread matches the fabric well. Start at a side seam and overlap your stitches when you get round to where you started.

**16** If you are making the version with the elasticated hem, topstitch round the hem, starting ¾in (2cm) after a side seam and using a ⅝in (1.5cm) seam allowance from the bottom edge of the top (see page 118). You can sew on the right or wrong side, but check the bobbin thread matches the fabric well. Sew all the way around the hem, but stop ¾in (2cm) before the seam so you have a 1⅝in (4cm) gap in your topstitching. Reverse stitch at the start and finish. Pin a safety pin on the end of the elastic and thread it through the gap you've left in the hem. You can put another safety pin on the other end of the elastic so it won't get lost inside the casing. Push the safety pin all the way around inside the casing, easing it through and releasing the bunched-up fabric every so often. Pull the safety pin out where you started and check the elastic is lying flat and not twisted inside the casing. You can join the two ends of the elastic together now with a safety pin and try on your top—this will give you an idea of where the elasticated hem will sit on your body, for example into your waist or right across your hips. If you're happy with the fit, overlap the two elastic ends by ⅝in (1.5cm) and fix them in place with a pin.

**17** Zigzag stitch across the elastic and reverse back over your stitching for extra strength. Pull the hem out to the sides and let the elastic disappear inside the casing. Topstitch across the gap in the hem, overlapping your original stitches by ⅜in (1cm) at the start and finish. If you're worried about the elastic twisting inside the casing, using a straight stitch, sew a straight line down the middle of your casing while stretching the elastic inside. Sew round the entire waistband and overlap your stitches by ⅜in (1cm) when you come round to where you started.

**18** To make a button loop at the back of the neck, use three strands of embroidery floss (thread). Thread them through the eye of a hand-sewing needle and knot both ends together (see page 124). Bring your needle up from underneath the neck facing to the right side at the corner, so that the knot is hidden. Make a loop by picking up a small amount of fabric lower down, about ⅜in (1cm) away from the corner, then go back and make an identical loop over the top, picking up a small amount of fabric each time. Put your needle into the loop and stretch the threads to make all the loops the same size. Check that your button can pass through the loop. To cover the thread loops, using your needle wind the thread around the loops until they are covered, pulling the thread tight as you go. When the loop is covered, secure your thread with a few small stitches at the top of the loop on the fabric. Push the thread to the wrong side of the facing and cut it off. Sew the button on the other side of the neck opening (see page 120), making sure that it is level with the loop. You can try this classic shape with different fabrics and even extend it to make a dress.

Skill level ✳✳

This is the best drawstring skirt ever! We don't want a load of fabric bunching round the front of a skirt but we do want it to be comfortable, easy to put on, and easy to wear. This combination of an elasticated back and a drawstring front is the answer and it looks great, too.

# Drawstring Skirt

## YOU WILL NEED

**For the skirt:** main fabric—see page 110 for amount required

**For the drawstring ties:** 2 pieces of fabric, each 2¼ x 25⅝in (5.5 x 65cm), or you can use ribbon

Iron-on interfacing, 1⅜ x 4⅜in (3.5 x 11cm)

1in- (2.5cm-) wide elastic: hold the elastic behind you, along the back of your waist from side to side with a slight stretch and cut it to this length

Matching sewing thread

Basic sewing kit (see page 5)

## FINISHED MEASUREMENTS

Custom size

## LEARN HOW TO

- Sew a buttonhole
- Make an elastic casing
- Create a drawstring
- Topstitch a double hem
- Thread elastic through a casing

**1** Follow the instructions on page 110 to calculate the amount of fabric you will need. If you are using two pieces of fabric, place them together with the right sides facing. Stitch them together down one of the short sides, using a seam allowance of ⅝in (1.5cm) (see page 118). To reinforce the seam, sew a row of zigzag stitching near the edge, then trim close to the zigzag (see page 119).

**3** To prepare the casing for the elastic, press a double hem (see page 121) on the top edge of the skirt fabric. First fold the top edge to the wrong side by ⅜in (1cm) and press, then fold it to the wrong side again by 1⅜in (3.5cm) and press. To press the double hem at the bottom of the skirt, fold the bottom edge to the wrong side by ⅜in (1cm) and press, then fold it to the wrong side by ⅝in (1.5cm) and press.

**2** Take one of the drawstring tie pieces and follow steps 1–2 on page 129 to make a folded strap. Topstitch (see page 114) down just the tucked-in side of the drawstring tie, a few millimeters from the edge. Repeat with the other drawstring tie piece.

*Tips* When you cut out patterned fabric, think about how the design will look joined up at the side seams and also what area of the design will be in the center of the skirt.

A small overall patterned fabric such as a ditsy floral will make matching up the design easier.

## To calculate the width of fabric required:

Take your waist measurement, multiply it by 1.5, and then add 1³⁄₁₆in (3cm) (for the seam allowance for both sides)

For example:
If your waist measurement was 33⅞in (86cm):
33⅞in (86cm) x 1.5 = 50¹³⁄₁₆in (129cm)
+ 1³⁄₁₆ (3cm) = 52in (132cm)
Width of fabric required = 52in (132cm)

## To calculate the length of fabric required:

Take the measurement from your waist (where you'd like your skirt to sit on your body) to where you'd like the skirt to finish. Then add a double hem of ⅜in (1cm) + 1⅜ (3.5cm) (for the elastic casing) and add a double hem of ⅜in (1cm) + ⅝in (1.5cm) for the bottom hem.

For example:
If you'd like the length of your skirt to be 21¾in (55cm):
21¾in (55cm) + waist casing for elastic (a double hem of ⅜in/1cm + 1⅜in/3.5cm) + bottom hem (a double hem of ⅜in/1cm + ⅝in/1.5cm) = 24½in (62cm)
Length of fabric required = 24½in (62cm)

Fabric dimensions required: 52 x 24½in (132cm x 62cm)

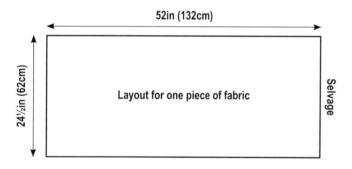

Below is the layout if you need to cut out the fabric in two pieces. Keep the width of the pieces equal so the side seams remain at each side of the skirt. The length of the fabric stays the same.

For example:
Waist measurement = 33⅞in (86cm) x 1.5 = 50¹³⁄₁₆in (129cm)
50¹³⁄₁₆in (129cm) divided by 2 = 25⁷⁄₁₆in (64.5cm) + seam allowance (⅝in/1.5cm + ⅝in/1.5cm) = 26¹¹⁄₁₆in (67.5cm) = width of each piece

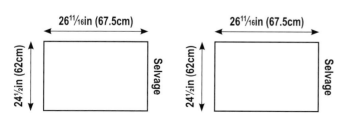

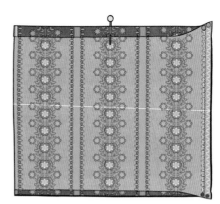

**4** Fold the skirt fabric in half, matching up the short sides. Pin down the short side, opening up the pressed double hems at the top and bottom so you won't sew over them. Sew down the short side with a ⅝in (1.5cm) seam allowance, reverse stitching at the start and finish (see page 115). To reinforce your seam, sew a row of zigzag stitching near the edge, then trim close to the zigzag. With the seam at one side and the fold at the other, use chalk to mark the top of the fold—this is the halfway point. Then measure and mark the center of the side of the skirt that is facing you and mark it with a pin through one single layer only and at a right angle to the top edge, so that the pin sticks out from the top edge.

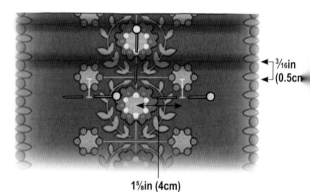

³⁄₁₆in (0.5cm)

1⅝in (4cm)

**5** Open out the first fold of the hem at the top of the skirt (the casing) in the area close to the central pin. Use a pen or chalk marker to mark two buttonholes (like a capital letter "I" and ⅝in/1.5cm in length) on the right side, each 1⅝in (4cm) away from the central pin and ³⁄₁₆in (0.5cm) down from the pressed crease of the double hem. The buttonholes should be ⅝in (1.5cm) long. If you have an automatic buttonhole function on your machine, choose a button with a diameter of ⅝in (1.5cm) to clamp into the back of the foot. It's best to consult your sewing machine manual to find out all the settings you must put in place to make a buttonhole on your machine (see page 130). Place a horizontal pin in the bottom of each of the marked buttonholes.

**6** Flip the skirt over to the wrong side and where you can see the pins, lay the interfacing with the rough (glue) side face down on the wrong side of the fabric. Check from the right side that the area where the buttonhole markings will be sewn is covered by interfacing. Remove the pins before you press the interfacing in place with a cool iron. This will reinforce the fabric for the buttonholes.

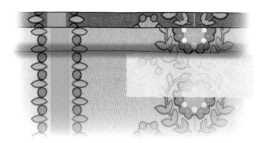

**7** On the right side of the fabric where the buttonhole markings are, place a pin in the bottom of each buttonhole marking again, to help you position the sewing-machine foot to start the buttonhole. Consult your sewing machine manual—some machines start stitching buttonholes at the bottom and others start at the top. Stitch each buttonhole and don't forget to reset your machine before the second one. When you come round to where you started, if the zigzag stitching is a bit sparse, without moving your sewing-machine foot you can sew over your existing stitches to make them thicker. Use a seam ripper to make a small hole in the center of the buttonhole and then use a sharp pair of small scissors to open up the buttonhole (see page 130). Place a pin at each end of the buttonhole to prevent you cutting your stitches. Trim off any bits of loose thread to neaten each buttonhole.

**8** Fold over the double hem casing at the top of the skirt to the wrong side along the crease lines. On the wrong side and starting from the side seam, topstitch all the way around the top hem using the left-hand side of the sewing-machine foot as your guide on the lower folded edge of the hem (see page 118). Overlap your stitches by ⅜in (1cm) when you get back to the beginning (see page 115). Make sure your bobbin thread matches your fabric well and that you sew below the buttonholes.

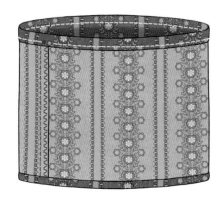

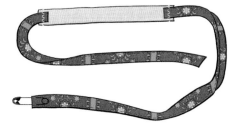

**9** Fabric-clip or pin one drawstring tie to one end of the elastic and the other tie to the other end of the elastic. Sew with zigzag stitch over the ends to join them, and reverse-stitch back over your stitches so it's extra secure. Pin a safety pin onto one end of the drawstring.

**10** Turn the skirt to the right side. Feed the safety pin into the casing at the top of the skirt through one of the buttonholes. When the elastic, which is a bit wider, comes to the buttonhole, fold the elastic in half to get it through. Push the safety pin all the way around so it comes out of the other buttonhole, then pull the drawstring out until the join of the elastic and drawstring tie is at the halfway point marked with chalk. Put a pin through all layers to secure it. Make sure the elastic isn't twisted inside the casing, and line up the other elastic and

drawstring join with the side seam on the skirt. Put a pin through all layers to secure it. Sew down across the elastic through all layers at the side seam, then reverse back over your stitches. Repeat to sew across the elastic at the halfway point, then reverse back over your stitches.

**11** Pin the double hem at the bottom of the skirt in place. Starting at a side seam, topstitch all around the hem on the right side using a ⅜in (1cm) seam allowance. Overlap your stitches by ⅜in (1cm) when you get back to where you started. To finish off the ends of the drawstring ties, you can either tie them in a knot at each end or attach a bead or pompom to each end. This drawstring skirt doesn't require a pattern so it's a great starting point for building up your confidence with dressmaking!

# WORKSHOP 1: Cutting Out and Pinning

## Using templates

There are four types of template in this book:

■ Some of the projects have templates in the back of the book. If the template is full-size, you can photocopy it or trace it onto paper. If the template at the back of the book is at 50%, photocopy it, using the 200% zoom button on the photocopier. If a template is at 25%, you will need to enlarge it by 400%. To do this, enlarge by 200% on a photocopier, and then enlarge that photocopy by another 200%. Cut out the template before you use it.

■ Some projects start with squares or rectangles of fabric. Use a ruler and a pencil to draw these, using a set square to draw the corners or use graph/dot and cross paper. You can draw the square or rectangle on paper first, then cut it out to make your own paper template or draw it directly onto your fabric.

■ Four of the projects—the Pet Bed, Reversible Tote, Duster Jacket, and Cross-back Apron—include diagrams at the back of the book. Use the measurements on the diagrams to draft out the templates on paper at 100%. The more complex diagrams include instructions to help you draw them out.

■ Some projects (such as the Foldable Coin Purse on page 66) have templates in the back of the book that you use as sewing guides rather than cutting guides. You will draw around the template onto your fabric and then sew directly on that line. Then follow the project instructions to carefully cut out around the shape, leaving a seam allowance and avoiding cutting through the sewn seam.

### What is the selvage?

The selvage is the finished edge of the fabric which runs down the length of the fabric. Fabric pattern designs usually run parallel to this edge.

If you are using a paper template, place it onto your fabric and pin it in place. In some projects, you will see a layout plan that shows you how to position the templates on a folded piece of fabric before you cut them out. When you fold your fabric, make sure the finished edges of the fabric (the selvages) are together. Pin your template onto the fabric parallel to the selvage and not at an angle. Some patterns

have a double-headed grainline arrow, which should lie parallel to the selvedge. Don't rely on the printed pattern on the fabric, such as a stripe or a repeat pattern, because it can often get distorted and not follow the true grainline.

Some projects, such as the Neck Tie on page 54, require the fabric to be cut on the diagonal or "bias-cut," which allows the fabric to have a natural stretch and fluidity. The template is laid at an angle of 45 degrees from the selvage so that the weave or print design will run diagonally. This is also useful for bias binding and it gives better drape qualities in garments.

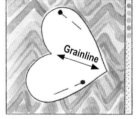

### Place to fold lines

When the grain line turns in at each end at right angles on the template, it means that the edge of the template that the arrows point to needs to be placed on the fold of the fabric. You cut around all other sides of the template except this one on the fold. You will end up with one big symmetrical fabric piece once the template is cut out.

### Transferring template notches

On some of the templates, you will see black triangles. These are called notches and they tell you where to position another piece of fabric when you assemble your project. To indicate the notch, either make a tiny snip into the triangle and your fabric or when instructed, mark it with a pen dot on the fabric in the same place.

## Mark-making: the "pin-and-mark" method

We often need to transfer other important markings onto our fabric from paper templates, such as the position of the magnetic clasp for the Glasses/Phone Case, or where you should overlap your Cozy Slipper top pieces (see page 49). You can transfer these markings by using a pin and your choice of marking tool, such as a pen or chalk marker. Choose a method that will mark your fabric the least amount while still allowing you to see the mark. Always test your marker on the fabric first.

**1** After cutting out your fabric, keep your paper template pinned onto it in position and push a pin through the template where the mark is.

**2** Carefully lift the paper template up, keeping the pin in place. Mark a dot underneath on your fabric with a pencil, pen, or chalk exactly where the pin goes into the fabric. You can mark several layers at one time with a long pin if you need to, just lift up the layers carefully while keeping the pin in place. If you mark on the right side of the fabric, make sure your mark gets covered or is within the seam allowance so it won't show.

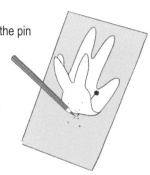

## Directional prints

Fabrics with a directional print can only be cut one way up. If you are using a fabric with a directional print, be careful to place your template on the fabric so that the print is going in the right direction from the top to the bottom of the template. You don't want your print upside down on your finished make! Note that you should not use directional prints for the following, because they have flip-over bag flaps, straps and/or visible linings: Tailor-made Top, Laptop Bag, Soft Plant Pots Covers (lining), Neck Ties, Crossbody Bag, Glasses/Phone Case (lining), Foldable Coin Purse, Bag Strap, Cosmetic Bag, Cross-back Apron.

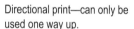
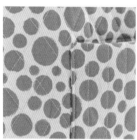

Directional print—can only be used one way up.

Non-directional print—can be used either way up.

## Cutting out the fabric

When using fabric scissors, cut with the lower blade touching the table. You get better results when you do big cuts farther up the blade than small snips with the tip of the blade, where it might not be so sharp. Move the fabric as you cut around—don't get in the habit of stretching or leaning over the table.

Some people prefer using a rotary cutter to cut out fabric, but these must be used with caution. Always use one with a ⅛–³⁄₁₆in (0.3–0.5cm) thick quilting ruler and a rotary mat, stand up when cutting to maintain an even pressure, and cut away from the body. Always retract the blade when it is not in use.

## Pinning templates to fabric before cutting out

When you are pinning your template to the fabric, place pins near the edge of the template (within the seam allowance, see page 118). This will avoid prick marks in your fabric (especially in suedette or polyester satin) and will prevent the paper template from lifting when you cut the fabric with scissors, which causes an inaccurate cut. When you've cut out your template, leave the template pinned on until you are ready to sew so you can identify the pattern pieces easily.

## Pinning to prepare for sewing

To prepare for sewing, always pin the fabrics together in a clockwise direction and more importantly, with the pin heads pointing to the direction you are sewing, so you can easily pull out the pins as you sew. This means they won't get stuck under the sewing-machine foot or break the needle if you sew over them by accident. Sometimes fabric is thick and fabric clips are easier to use. Just remember that you can't sew as near to them as you can with pins—as they fasten so well to the fabric, they can force you to sew askew if you don't remove them in time.

# WORKSHOP 2 : Sewing Skills

## Using a sewing machine

Always refer to the manufacturer's instructions to thread your sewing machine and work out the correct tension. Before starting to sew up your project, practice on a spare piece of fabric, preferably the same as your project fabric. When we sew, we mostly use two layers of fabric, so double up your practice fabric, check the stitches are even on both sides, and change the tension or stitch length if you need to. Whenever you change your thread, check your sewing on a spare piece of fabric. Once you can sew a lovely straight line, you can start adding some curves and corners (see page 116) to your skill set.

**1** Refer to the manufacturer's instructions to wind up the bobbin and thread up the machine with a full bobbin and spool thread on top. Always thread up with the presser foot lifted and the needle raised. As per your manufacturer's instructions, bring the bobbin thread up to the top to join the spool thread, leaving a long tail of bobbin and spool thread measuring about 8in (20cm) from the needle. Pull the thread tails toward the back of the machine before you start to stitch, to avoid your needle unthreading. Check that you have selected the correct stitch in the size you'd like to use (see below).

**2** Raise the presser foot and the needle and place your fabric underneath. Line up the edge of your fabric with the side of the presser foot or one of the markings on the machine plate (see page 118), depending what size you want your seam allowance to be.

**3** Lower the presser foot. Start to stitch by pressing on the foot pedal. Always keep your fingers well away from the needle when your foot is on the pedal! Keep the edge of the fabric lined up with the seam guide you are using. Gently guide the fabric away from you with both hands, holding the fabric at the front, and allow the fabric to move out at the back. Don't pull or push the fabric, as the machine has "feed dogs" that will do the work for you.

**4** When you come to the end, reverse stitch (see opposite). Check that the needle is out of the fabric and at its highest point, so you can see the thread take-up lever pop out at the top. If the needle is not at its highest point, use the hand wheel to raise it, (always bring the handwheel toward you) then raise the presser foot and pull the fabric away to the left. Cut the threads close to the fabric, and leave the thread tails to hang out of the back of the sewing machine, so you are ready to sew again.

## Sewing key

On some of the artworks, you will see colored dots that show you where to sew.

 Start sewing at the green dot.

 Stop sewing at the red dot.

## Machine stitches

You only need a sewing machine with straight stitch (2.5 on your stitch length indicator), zigzag stitch, and buttonhole stitch. But other stitches can also be useful, such as multi-step zigzag and blind hemming stitch. Topstitch is just a name we give to a longer straight stitch (around 3-4 on your stitch length indicator). You can make your stitches longer by using the stitch length dial on your sewing machine. Topstitch is meant to be seen on the outside of your project. It looks better longer and as it's decorative, the stitches don't have to be so short and strong.

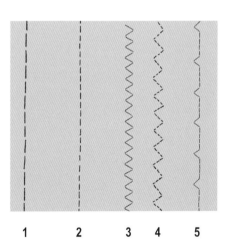

1    2    3    4    5

1. Topstitch: stitch length 3
2. Straight stitch: stitch length 2.5
3. Zigzag
4. Multi-step zigzag
5. Blind hem

## Reverse stitch

In the projects, I often say "reverse stitch at the start and finish." This means that the seam needs to be strong at both ends so it won't come undone. On your machine, you will have a reverse stitch lever or a button. To do a reverse stitch, just hold it down as you sew backward for a few seconds, then release it and continue sewing forward.

When the instructions tell you to start with a reverse stitch, position your needle ⅜in (1cm) in from where you want to start sewing, for example at a turning gap. Start by reverse-stitching ⅜in (1cm) to that turning gap, then sew forward on your way.

To finish with a reverse stitch (such as at the end of a seam), sew to where you need to stop then hold down the lever or button as you sew backward by about ⅜in (1cm). Remove your project there, and cut off your threads. You don't always need to reverse stitch when you sew, but if you are unsure, sew a reverse stitch anyway!

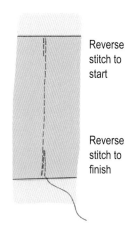

Reverse stitch to start

Reverse stitch to finish

## Sewing all the way around

One example where you don't need to do a reverse stitch is when you are sewing all the way around a circle, square, or rectangle, the top of a bag, or a strap. Here, you just need to sew around to the beginning of your seam and overlap your stitches by about ⅜in (1cm). This will be enough to secure the stitches.

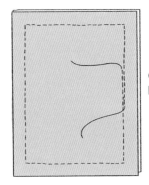

Overlapping by ⅜in (1cm)

## Handwheel stitches

When you want more precision and your foot pedal control isn't slow enough, stop a few stitches early and turn the handwheel forward on your sewing machine to do a few stitches. The handwheel is also useful when you need to sew through thick layers of fabric and you need a helping hand to get over the bulkiness while also pulling the fabric gently from the back.

## Free arm sewing

The extension table can usually be slid off the machine to the left to reveal the free-arm capability of your machine. This will enable you to sew tubular shapes such as sleeves, cuffs, or the Soft Plant Pot Covers on page 19. You slide your project underneath, which makes it easier to guide the fabric under the needle and sew all the way in a round, avoiding accidentally catching other parts of your fabric.

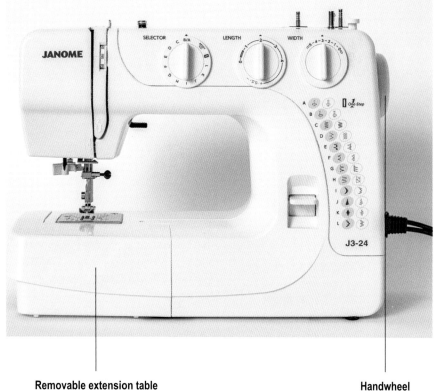

Removable extension table

Handwheel

## Sewing corners

When you turn a corner, you want to be accurate so that your corner is sharp. As you come close to the corner, lift your foot away from the foot pedal and use the handwheel to do those final stitches to the corner. This allows you more control, as stopping right where you need to using your foot pedal isn't easy.

Stop sewing and leave the needle deep in the fabric, lift your presser foot up, and turn your fabric in the direction you want to go. This is called pivoting on the needle, and it keeps your fabric in place as you turn. Then put the presser foot down and continue to sew using the foot pedal. If you find it difficult to know where to pivot, get to where you think you should turn, leave the needle down, and pivot. Then check that the fabric is level with the sewing-machine foot or your throat plate guideline depending on what seam allowance you're using. If it

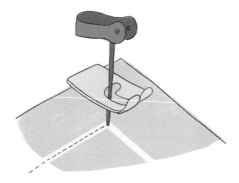

isn't and you've turned too soon, just pivot back, do one or two handwheel stitches and pivot again, checking your seam allowance is correct to continue sewing. With practice you will know where to do the pivot. If you've sewn beyond the correct pivot position, then take your project out and start sewing the corner again. If you leave those overhanging stitches, they will get cut through if you need to trim the corner and the stitching will unravel.

Both seam allowances are the same along the corner.

## Sewing curves

If you can get your sewing machine to sew very slowly by lightly pressing on the foot pedal, you can probably sew a gentle curve in one go without stopping. If you're sewing a tight curve you will need to pivot, so leave your needle in the fabric, lift up your presser foot, and turn the fabric slightly so the presser foot is pointing where you next want to sew. You can pivot as many times as you like: no one will ever know how many times you've pivoted to get that perfect curve. Neat stitching is our goal, after all! For extra guidance, you can follow a drawn line or dots that you've marked with a ruler (see page 118) or use the right-hand side of your foot as a guide on the edge of the fabric (see page 118) as you go around the curve. You can also use a circular object such as a mug to draw the curve before you sew it (such as in the Garden Kneeler project on page 26).

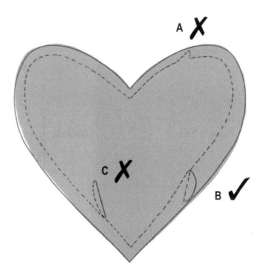

If you find yourself straying from where you want to sew, just moving your needle back on track will form a long stitch called a float and this will create an unwanted hole (A). Instead, lift your presser foot and needle and move your fabric to position the needle back down where you started to stray, then continue sewing (B). If you have strayed more than ⅜in (1cm), then it's best to lift

up your presser foot and needle, cut your thread, and start sewing again just before the place where you strayed, overlapping your stitches. Try to avoid straying inside the shape with your sewing (C), as this will affect the outline and the project will look bunched up when you turn it through to the right side. If this happens, it's best to unpick your stitches (see opposite).

## Undoing stitches when you have gone wrong

If you've sewn in the wrong place, you can easily undo your stitches with a seam ripper. Push the pointed end up through the stitches that you want to remove and cut them with the sharp "U-shaped" blade. Repeat this along the stitching line, then tidy up by pulling the loose threads out of the fabric. Often, it's easier to open up the seam and cut the stitches between the layers.

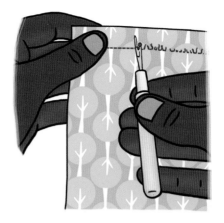

## Pressing

Pressing is different to ironing. Ironing gets rid of wrinkles and pressing puts creases in! With pressing, you don't slide the iron over the fabric—you hold it still for a moment to fix the crease or push the stitches into the fabric, flattening any puckers. For a professional finish, press seams well at every step of a project; it will make such a difference to the final result. I use a mini travel iron or if I don't want to keep the iron on, I use a seam roller (see page 5). Pressing curved seams is easier using a tailor's ham. The rounded ends of the ham help to shape seams while pressing and can help get the iron into awkward spots, too.

### Setting seams

Setting the seams is when you press your stitched seam flat (as it was sewn) before pressing it open (see above right) or to one side, or turn your project to the right side. It smooths out any puckers, wrinkles, or uneven stitches which can be caused by tension issues. You can do this to all seams before you continue to the next step.

### Pressing seams open

Often when you have stitched a seam, for example between patchwork pieces (see page 126), the project instructions tell you to press it open. To do this, run a seam roller or the tip of an iron along the seam so the two edges of fabric open out to lie flat on either side of the seam.

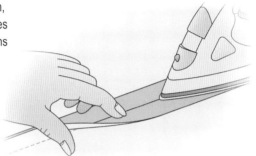

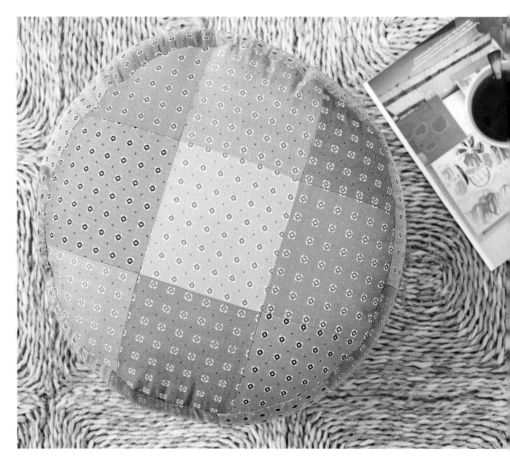

# WORKSHOP 3 : Seams, Hems, Mitered Corners, and Darts

## Seam allowances and sewing a seam

A seam is a line of stitches, usually straight stitches, that connect two pieces of fabric. The seam allowance is the distance between the edge of the fabric and your seam. You need to sew evenly to keep the seam allowance the same so all the pieces will fit together. The instructions will give you a seam allowance to use.

There are several ways to sew a straight seam on your machine. You can line up the edge of the fabric with the presser foot, or use one of the guide lines marked on the throat plate of your machine. Always try to sew in a clockwise direction, with the bulk of your fabric to the left of needle, so your project is not all bunched up in the throat space (the space between the needle and motor).

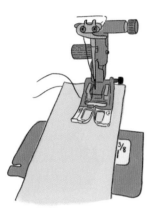

**1 Using your machine's throat plate seam guide:** Line the edge of your fabric up with the ⅜in (1cm) guide on your machine to give you the standard seam allowance used for the projects in this book. You can also stick colored or washi tape on your machine as your guide.

**2 Using the right-hand side of the foot, with the needle in the center:** Some of the projects tell you to use the right-hand side of the foot as your guide for sewing a seam. Line up the edge of the fabric with the right-hand edge of your foot. This gives you a seam allowance of about ¼in (7mm).

**3 Using the right-hand side of the foot, with the needle position moved to the left:** This makes the seam allowance of about ⅜in (1cm). Use the dial or button on your machine to move the needle to the left (make sure your needle is up)—often it means switching to the next stitch on your dial or display.

If you have trouble keeping your seam allowance even, especially around a curve, use a hem gauge or ruler to mark dots at intervals that are the same distance from the edge of the fabric as your seam allowance. Then sew through your dots.

*Note* The projects in this book use a ⅜in (1cm) seam allowance unless stated otherwise.

## Reinforcing seams

After you sew a straight stitch, a zigzag stitch can be used as a seam finish to help prevent the fabric edges fraying and to strengthen the seam. If you use a larger seam allowance of ⅝in (1.5cm) (this is the standard seam allowance for dressmaking patterns—see the Duster Jacket on page 101 and Drawstring Skirt on page 109), then you will have enough room to fit in a zigzag stitch. Position the left-hand side of your sewing-machine foot on your row of straight stitches, then sew a zigzag stitch. Trim close to the zigzag to neaten.

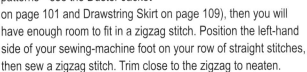

To add more stability to your seams and strengthen them, sometimes you need to sew a second line of stitching (using the same straight stitch) directly on top of your first row. This is often done on corners or when you need to snip deep into a curve or a "V" shape.

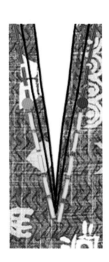

## Reducing bulk in seams

### Clipping corners

When you sew a corner, you need to clip into the fabric up to your stitches, being careful not to cut through them. This means your fabric will lie flat and not bunch up when you turn it to the right side.

For an inward corner, snip as far into the angle and as close to your stitching as you can.

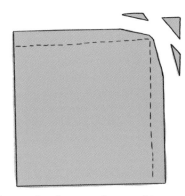

For an outward corner, snip across it to remove excess fabric.

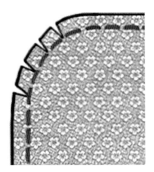

### Clipping curves

When you sew a curve, you need to clip into the fabric up to your stitches at intervals, with lots of snips if it's a sharp curve. Use the tip of a sharp pair of scissors, so you don't cut through your stitches. This will make the fabric lay flat, giving you a smooth curve when you turn it to the right side.

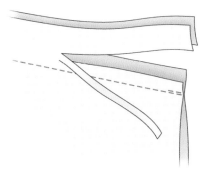

### Grading seams

Also known as layering seams, grading involves trimming the seam allowances to graduated widths to reduce bulk in the layers and to give a flatter appearance. Trim the narrowest seam allowance down to no less than ³⁄₁₆in (0.5cm). If you are using a fabric that frays, don't trim too closely to your stitches.

## French seams

French seams create a neat finish, concealing all the raw edges of the fabric. This technique is useful with sheer, lightweight fabrics and fabrics that fray a lot, but you can also use it on a medium-weight cotton. It is often used in nightwear and children's clothing because the encased seam can be softer on the skin. This method can be used when the seam allowance is ⅝in (1.5cm).

**1** With the wrong sides of the fabrics together, sew down the edge with the right-hand side of the sewing-machine foot on the edge of the fabric (to sew with a ¼in/7mm seam allowance, see page 118). Trim the raw edge to about ⅛in (3mm).

**2** Turn back the fabric along the seam so the right sides are touching and press it in place. Sew down the edge with the right-hand side of the sewing-machine foot on the folded edge of the fabric (to sew with a ¼in/7mm seam allowance).

**3** When you turn the piece to the right side, you shouldn't see any loose threads sticking out from the seam. If you do, this is because your second seam wasn't deep enough or you didn't trim the seam enough, but you can just sew the seam again about ⅛in (a few millimeters) away from your first line of stitching.

## Making sure a seam is pressed to one side

Sometimes you need to press a seam so it's right on the edge, for example for the Bag Strap (see page 64) or for a French seam. The easiest way to do this is roll the seam gently back and forth between your fingers so you can see the stitches, encouraging the seam to sit right on the edge. Press the seam once you've rolled each section.

## Matching up seams

Often, we need to match up different fabric pieces at their seams. For example, when we sew patchwork (see page 126), any mismatching really stands out, especially if the pieces have contrasting colors.

With the right sides together, put a pin through the middle of one seam. Then push it through the middle of the other seam at the same distance from the edge.

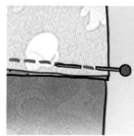

Then bring the pin forward, pushing it through both seams again but lower down to fix in place. When you come to sew the pieces together, sew as close as you can to the pin before removing it. By using this method to match pieces up at their seams, you can achieve a top-notch professional finish!

# Hems

A hem is a way of neatening the raw edge of the fabric by turning up the edge and sewing it in place. You would sew a hem on the bottom of a skirt or the top of a bag, for example.

### Sewing a hem

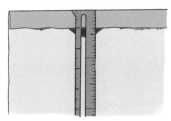
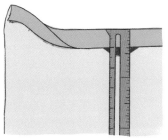
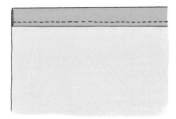

**1** To sew a simple double-turned hem, first fold the raw edge of your fabric over to the wrong side by ⅝in (1.5cm) and then press.

**2** Fold this edge over to the wrong side again by ⅝in (1.5cm), and then press again.

**3** Then sew a straight stitch along the hem, using the right-hand side of the foot as your guide on the folded edge. You might like to try a topstitch in a contrast thread to give your garment a distinctive look.

# Mitered corners

This technique is used in the Napkins and Table Runner project on page 8 to create a neat, flat, right-angled corner. These instructions will create a 1in (2.5cm) deep double hem with a mitered corner.

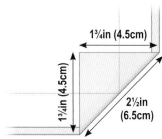
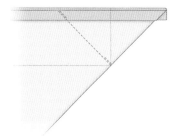
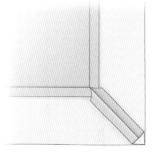

**1** Follow step 3 on page 10 to press the double hem all around the napkin. Working from the wrong side, open out the 1in (2.5cm) fold at a corner. Mark two pen dots on the folded edges, each 1¾in (4.5cm) from the tip of the corner. You can either fold the corner at these points and press the line in, or use a ruler and pencil or chalk marker to draw a line joining the dots. The line should be 2½in (6.5cm).

**2** Turn back the corner on itself with the right sides of the fabric together. Make sure the two folded edges are level with each other. Starting from the folded side, sew on top of your pen line (or crease) with reverse stitch at the start and finish (see page 115).

**3** After sewing, trim the seam to about ³⁄₁₆in (0.5cm) and cut the tiny corner off. Press the seam allowance open. Then turn the napkin to the right side and push out the corner with a pointer. Repeat with the other corners, making sure the seams are pressed flat inside the mitered corners.

# Darts

Using darts is a way of shaping your flat fabric by pinching in a wedge of fabric and sewing it in place. Always sew from the wide end to the narrow end. To secure the end of the dart, you can either leave long thread tails so you can tie a secure double knot (and then cut the tails off leaving ⅜in/1cm) or you can do a reverse stitch (see page 115). The important thing is that there are no puckers showing on the right side at the pointed end of the dart.

# WORKSHOP 4 : Building on Your Skills

With sewing, we like to make everything look neat, so we often sew a project together on the "wrong side" of the fabric and then turn the project through to the right side. I call this the inside-out method. The wrong side of the fabric is the back of the fabric, or the side without a print if you're using a patterned fabric. Some fabrics look very similar on the back and front—for these, use the side that's duller and less smooth as the wrong side. Also look at the pinholes (which are created by a factory finishing process) on the selvage (see page 112)—if they are neat and smooth then that is the wrong side of the fabric.

## Turning gaps

After sewing two pieces together with the right sides of the fabrics touching and the wrong sides facing outward, you will need a gap in the stitching to be able to turn your project inside out, through to the right side. This is called a turning gap. The length of the gap depends on the project. For example, to stuff the Pet Bed (see page 22), you need the gap to be big enough for your fingers to get in and push the fiberfill stuffing into all the far corners of your project.

To sew and then close a turning gap:

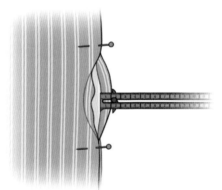

**1** Sew the pieces together, reverse stitching at the start and finish (see page 115) and leaving the turning gap unsewn.

**2** Turn the project through to the right side by pulling and pushing the fabric out through the turning gap. Put two pins in at right angles to the edge of the fabric to mark where the gap is. Tuck the seam allowance of each side of the turning gap to the inside. Here the seam allowance is ⅜in (1cm).

**3** Sew along the edge of the turning gap to close it, ⅜in (1cm) beyond the start and finish of the gap. Reverse stitch at each end.

## Linings

For projects that have linings, the turning gap should be in the lining so it won't show. For example, for the Glasses/Phone case (see page 72) we leave a turning gap in the bottom of the lining and then turn the project to the right side through the turning gap.

The seam allowance of the turning gap is then tucked to the inside and pinned in place, and then sewn closed (see opposite). Alternatively, you can hand sew the turning gap closed (see page 125).

## Patch pockets

The neatest way to make a patch pocket is to make one that is lined.

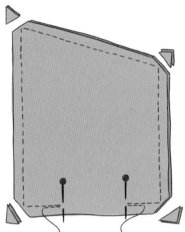  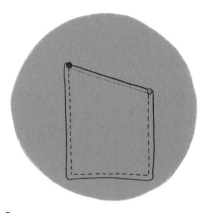

**1** After cutting two identical pocket pieces, place them together with the right sides touching. Pin and then sew the two pieces together, using the right-hand side of the foot as your guide (see page 118). Reverse stitch (see page 115) at the start and finish and leave a turning gap on the bottom edge of the pocket. Put two pins in at right angles to mark where the gap should be. Pivot (see page 116) at the corners to make them sharp. Trim the corners and if your pocket is curved, clip the curves (see page 119). Before turning the pocket to the right side, set the seams with the iron (see page 117).

**2** Pull the fabric out through the turning gap to turn the pocket to the right side. Use a pointer to push out all the corners. Give the pocket a press, rolling out the seams with your fingers so neither side is showing more on one side. Topstitch (see page 114) along the top edge of the pocket, using the right-hand side of the foot on the edge of the pocket as your guide. Tuck in the raw edges of the turning gap and fix them with a pin.

**3** Pin the pocket in place on your project. Sew around the three sides of the pocket, starting at the green dot and finishing at the red dot. Reverse stitch at the green and red dots. You will sew over and close the turning gap when you sew across the bottom.

## Understitching

Understitching, like topstitching, is done from the right side of the fabric. It is stitched a fraction of an inch (a few millimeters) away from the seamline to keep a facing or lining in place on the inside where it should be and to give a neat, crisp edge. If the layers are bulky you can grade the seam allowances (see page 119), and clip into them if they are curved. With the right side of the facing on top, topstitch close to the seamline, stitching through the facing and the seam allowances at the same time.

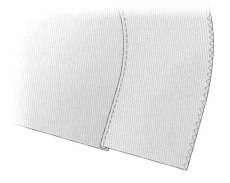

# WORKSHOP 5: Hand Sewing

Even if you're using a sewing machine, sometimes you'll need to do a bit of hand sewing to finish off your project. Whether it's to close a turning or stuffing gap or sew on a button, you'll need to perfect a neat hand-sewn stitch.

## Threading a needle
In the projects, we use a double thread because it's stronger and won't come undone.

**1** Pull off a length of thread, the length of your arm, from the reel. Then continue by pulling off the same amount of thread again to double it—that way your arm will always be long enough to pull the thread through as you sew.

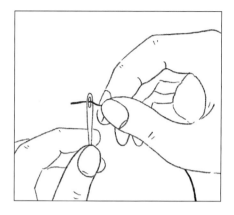

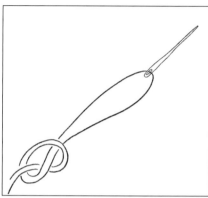

**2** Use a needle that has the smallest eye you can thread yourself—it will go through fabric far more easily than a chunky needle.

**3** To thread the needle, hold about ¼in (0.5cm) of the thread end between your thumb and forefinger and move the needle to take the thread through its eye. If the thread is too fluffy, cut off the end with a sharp pair of scissors. Alternatively, fold the end of the thread to form a little loop, squash it between your thumb and forefinger, and push this tiny loop through the eye. Pull the loop through until it becomes one strand and you only have a single thread going through the eye of the needle.

**4** With the two thread ends together, tie a knot as near to the end as you can.

## Securing your thread
Make one small stitch in your fabric and pull until there's a ⅜in (1cm) tail remaining, then put your needle through that loop and pull tight. You can tuck the tail of the knot under your stitches as you start to sew.

## Securing your stitches/fastening off
When you want to finish (fasten off), do two small stitches in the same place. From there, push the needle into the seam, and then pop it up about an inch (2.5cm) further down the seam. This way, there will be a long tail running along underneath so when you cut the thread off, your stitches won't unravel.

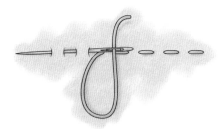

## Running stitch/basting (tacking)

You can use this simple "in and out" stitch to temporarily join two or more pieces of fabric together when you need extra stability with thick layers or slippery fabric, or when need to hold something temporarily in place such as a zipper when pins would get in the way. Use a single or double thread in a contrasting color to your sewing-machine thread. When you sew these stitches, keep clear of the seam allowance so when you've machine-sewn, you can easily remove them.

Secure the thread at the back of your fabric and push the needle to the front. Start by pushing the needle down through the fabric a little way along, then bring it back up through the fabric a little further along. Repeat to form a row of even stitches like a dashed line.

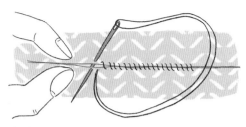

## Whipstitch

Use this stitch to close up a gap. Tuck the two raw edges of the fabric to the inside along the gap, and pin in place. After securing your thread, take the needle and thread over to the back and, while pinching the gap together between your thumb and forefinger, insert your needle from the back through to the front and pull up.

Continue along the opening by always bringing the needle from the back to the front. The smaller the stitches you can make, the better. If you're using fleece fabric, pull your stitches up tightly so the thread will sink into the fabric and be less visible.

## Ladder stitch

Ladder stitch is used when you want a discreet and invisible stitch to close an opening. So it's perfect for pillow or toy making, closing a lining, or repairing a seam. Fold in the seam allowance along the gap, securing the thread on one side of the gap. Bring the needle up through the fold of one of the seam allowances at A, then take it straight across the gap to B. Make a tiny stitch through the folded edge and bring it back to the front at C. Pull up these stitches so they are hidden and continue sewing another few "rungs" and then pull those up. Continue until the gap is closed and fasten off your thread.

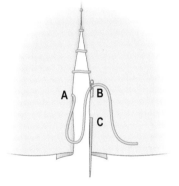

## Slipstitch

Slipstitch is a discreet stitch used to close or repair a seam, hem garments, finish a collar or waistband, or attach binding (see page 87 of the Cosmetics Bag). Use this stitch when you want the stitching to be hidden.

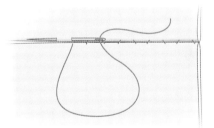

Working from right to left, secure your thread with a double stitch in the fold. Pick up a tiny stitch in the fabric opposite, put your needle into the fold of the hem, and run the needle inside that fold for about ¼in (6mm), popping out to make a tiny stitch in the fabric opposite. Enter the hem's fold with your needle and repeat the stitches. Pull up your stitches a little so they sink into the fabric.

## Tangles

Sometimes thread forms a loop while you are sewing and a slipknot is created, so watch out for these as you sew. When this happens, you'll need to remove the knot because it won't look good in among all your stitches. When a looped knot appears, stop sewing and put your needle into the loop. Pull on either side of your double thread in turn. One of the sides should make the knot shrink and then pop! The knot disappears as if by magic!

# WORKSHOP 6: Patchwork and Quilting

## Patchwork

Patchwork is the technique of sewing together small pieces of fabric to create something new and better. It's an excellent way of using up fabric scraps and thinking of the planet by recycling. Patchwork designs are made up of regular shapes such as squares, hexagons, or rectangular strips, that are cut out of fabric and then sewn together in a geometric pattern. It's important to sew straight and regular seams, as the pieces must all be sewn in the same way so they fit together. Patchwork designs are often sewn up in pairs of shapes, and then the pairs are sewn together and so on. Always follow the instructions in your project, which will tell you the order to sew up your shapes, and whether the seams should be pressed open or to one side.

A patchwork quilt can grow to become quite a big project, so the designs are broken down into bite-size pieces such as 12 x 12in (30 x 30cm) squares or "blocks." A bed quilt, for example, could be made up of 60 blocks! The French Press Jacket on page 34 is an ideal project to start you off on your patchwork journey.

These steps show you how to make a nine-patch square for the Pouffe on page 28, but the same method (with more squares) is used to sew the patchwork pieces for the French Press Jacket.

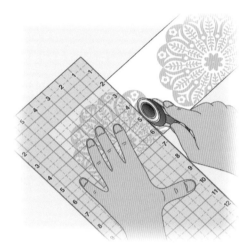

**1** To draw your patchwork pieces, use a ruler for straight lines and a set square for corners so they are right angles. If you're going to cut out lots of the same shape, you can make a cardboard template to draw around onto your fabric.

To help you, you can place a transparent quilting ruler over the top of your template and use a rotary cutter (see page 113) to cut out the squares.

With this method you can cut through a few layers at one time to save time. Alternatively, just mark each of the corners of the square with a dot, use a ruler to join the dots, and then use either scissors or a quilting ruler and a rotary cutter to cut them out. You could also use the lined grid in centimetres and/or inches on your cutting mat to cut accurate squares.

**2** Place your squares in your chosen arrangement. Here, a nine-patch square is being made.

**3** Place the middle square in the bottom row of your arrangement onto the bottom left-hand-side square, with their right sides facing. Pin and then sew them together along the right-hand edge, using the right-hand side of your sewing-machine foot as your guide on the edge of the fabric (see page 118). This will give you an accurate ¼in (7mm) seam allowance, and accuracy and consistency are important with patchwork. Repeat to sew the third square in the bottom row to the other side of the middle square (as shown here). Press the seams as per your project instructions. Repeat this process with the remaining two rows.

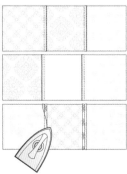

**4** Place the three sewn rows of squares on the table with the wrong side facing up. Press the seams on rows 1 and 3 to the right and the seams on row 2 to the left.

**5** Place rows 1 and 2 together with the right sides touching and match up all the seams with a pin (see page 120). Don't worry if you haven't quite matched them up exactly—no one will notice, and a little imperfection shows it's handmade. Sew the pieces together, again using the right-hand side of the foot as your guide on the edge of the fabric. Sew right up to the pins that are matching your seams together before removing them. Sew row 3 to the other side of row 2 in the same way. Press the seams on the back of your patchwork piece as per your project's instructions.

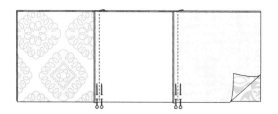

## Quilting

Quilting is a method of stitching layers of fabric together to give your projects extra softness and puffiness. It can be used on blankets as well as bags and clothing. Patchwork and quilting are often combined together. After you have sewn your patchwork "blocks" together, you would make a "quilt sandwich" with backing fabric, batting (wadding), and the patchwork design on top. You then stitch them together through all three layers.

You can also just do the quilting part to give your projects extra texture—all you need is some batting or fusible fleece. Think about your choice of thread color for your quilting stitches. The thread can be bright or contrasting so it stands out, or it can match your fabric and be understated.

To get that padded look, you need to sew through some batting (wadding) underneath your fabric. The best material to use on small projects is fusible fleece, which is thick enough to give you the quilted look but can also be ironed in place. The adhesive side is rough and bobbly and this is ironed onto the wrong side of the fabric. A walking foot is very useful for quilting or sewing any multi layers that are thick or slippery. It evenly feeds the top and bottom fabrics over the feed dogs separately. This prevents any shifting or puckering that would occur with a general-purpose presser foot.

There are four ways to create the quilted effect:

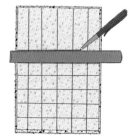

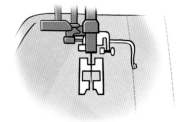

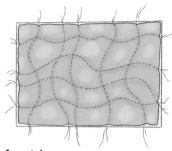

**Drawing out a grid to follow:**
Mark a grid on the wrong side of your project (on the fusible fleece) so it won't be seen. The easiest way to mark out parallel lines for a grid is to use the width of your ruler as a guide. If you need to mark the right side of the fabric, use an erasable pen, chalk, or mark creases with a hera marker–but first test it on a scrap piece of fabric to make sure the marks will come off. Once you have marked your lines, stitch over them using a topstitch (see page 114).

**Using a quilting guide bar:**
On most machines, the presser foot will accommodate a quilting guide bar, which is a right-angled piece of metal that slides into the back of your foot holder. First sew a few guidelines. For example, with the Zippered Pillow on page 14, you sew from corner to corner and then follow those lines with your guide bar. Decide on the width of your rows by adjusting the guide bar and then as you stitch, keep the guide bar on your marked line or previous stitch line, keeping the foot straight so your rows are parallel.

**Go freestyle:**
If you prefer, you can stitch curvy lines on the right side of your fabric instead of drawing a grid to follow!

**Following a patchwork or fabric design:**
On the right side of your fabric, you can sew your quilting stitch lines by following the horizontal and/or vertical seam lines you've created with your patchwork. You can also follow the designs of the fabric.

# WORKSHOP 7: Bag-making Skills and Fastenings

As well as being very satisfying to make, bag projects introduce you to a large range of techniques but on a small scale. You can start with simple bags, then add more features such as pockets, zippers, or linings as you expand your skills. Make the exact bag for what you need!

## Boxed corners

A bag needs a flat base to give it volume and stability, and so it can stand up on its own. To do this, we sew across the bottom corners.

**1** Follow the project instructions to sew the side seams and bottom seam (if there is one—the bottom may be folded instead) of your bag. Make sure the bag is inside out, with the wrong side of the fabric facing outward. Take hold of one corner of your bag from the inside, push your finger right in the corner, and flatten it out so it's pointed. To make sure you create an even (isosceles) triangle, put a pin through the middle of the side seam to line it up with the pressed crease or seam along the bottom of the bag.

**2** Using a ruler, draw a line across the base of the triangle. The project instructions will tell you what length the base should be, for example, 2⅜in (6cm). Pin the corner and then sew along your drawn line. Reverse stitch at the start and the finish (see page 115). If your fabric is delicate and likely to fray, you can leave the triangles as they are, or if they're large and bulky, you can trim them.

## Tube straps

The easiest way to make a strap or handle for a bag is to make a tube.

**1** Fold a rectangle of fabric in half and sew down the long side, reverse stitching at each end (see page 115). You can turn it to the right side by pulling it inside out by hand, but if it's a long tube, you may need help. Pin a safety pin on one end, through the side so it doesn't tear the raw edge.

**2** Push the safety pin down inside the tube, then pull and push the safety pin along through the fabric tunnel. The fabric may get scrunched up at the start, but you can help it by pulling and releasing those bunched-up gathers so you can continue.

**3** When the safety pin has emerged at the top, pull the rest of fabric through to the right side. Remove the pin. Press the strap with the seam at the side or in the middle. You can also topstitch (see page 114) close to each edge to give a professional finish.

You can also turn a tube through a gap left in the middle of the tube. This is useful when the tube is particularly long.

**1** Fold the rectangle in half, bringing the long raw edges together. Starting from each end, sew down the long raw edge, leaving a gap in the middle.

**2** Pin a safety pin onto the short end and push it inside the fabric tube until it comes out through the gap in the long side. Repeat to pin the safety pin onto the other short end and pull it through the gap in the long side.

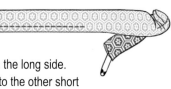

You can also use the blunt end of a knitting needle or chopstick to push the closed end of a fabric strap inside itself. Open up the seam at the end and push the chopstick into that end. Keep pushing it inside the tube and continue pushing the needle or chopstick through until the closed end of the fabric tube pops out of the open end.

Sometimes you need a neat, finished edge to your strap. Before sewing it and turning it to the right side, press ⅜in (1cm) of the short end to the wrong side of the fabric. Sew over the pressed fold when you sew down the side of the strap.

## Folded straps

To make firmer straps, you can fold them so you have four layers of fabric. This method is also used when fabric is too thick to be turned through.

**1** Fold the rectangle of fabric in half, bringing its long raw edges together, and press the fold so you have a central crease. Bring the outside edges into the central fold so that they meet in the middle and press in place.

**2** Fold the piece in half again so that you have four layers and press (or fix in place with fabric clips). Topstitch (see page 114) near each long edge to finish. You can leave the short edges unfinished because they're usually sewn into and hidden in the seam.

## Fastenings

### Sewing on buttons

There are two types of buttons—one with holes (two or four) and one with a shank (a loop). Buttons can be used as decorations or to hold things closed. Thread your needle with a double thread (see page 124) for extra strength.

#### Buttons with holes

**1** Mark the place where you want the button to go. Push the needle up from the back of the fabric and sew a few small stitches in this place.

**2** Bring the needle up through one of the button's holes, holding the button with the other hand. Push the needle down through the second hole and the fabric. Bring it back up through the fabric and then the first hole. Repeat five or six times. Make sure you go up and down through the button's holes so the thread doesn't loop around the side of the button. If your button has four holes, use all four of them to make either a cross or parallel pattern. Then wrap the thread around the threads beneath the button a few times, pulling the thread tight. Finish with a few small stitches on the back of the fabric and trim the thread.

#### Shank buttons

A shank button has a small loop on the back. These buttons don't lay flat on the fabric, and they are good for fastenings with loops (such as for the Tailor-made Top on page 104) and buttonholes in thicker fabric. Mark the position of the button on the fabric. Push the needle up from the back of the fabric and sew a few small stitches. Bring the needle through the loop on the back of the button, take the needle down through the fabric, then bring the needle up on the other side of the loop. Repeat five or six times. Then wrap the thread around the threads beneath the button a few times, pulling the thread tight. Finish with a few small stitches on the back of the fabric and trim the thread.

## Buttonholes

Consult your sewing machine manual to find out all the settings you must put in place to make a buttonhole. You may have a manual four-step buttonhole feature where you have to

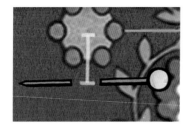

choose the stitches at every stage. Alternatively, you might have an automatic buttonhole foot where you place your button in the foot and it makes the buttonhole to fit that button. The important thing to do is practice, as it can be tricky to sew the buttonhole in the correct position. Mark out the position with a pen or chalk marker. Here, a pin has been placed through the bottom of the marking, but you don't need to do this unless the project tells you to.

Sometimes the button can be too big for the automatic buttonhole foot, so you will need to choose a manual method. Alternatively, the buttonhole that the machine automatically makes might be too big for the button,

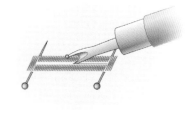

so you would need to choose a smaller button to put into the foot. You want the button to have some resistance when going through the buttonhole, so it doesn't come undone too easily. When cutting open a buttonhole, use a seam ripper and place a pin at either end of the buttonhole to prevent you cutting past the buttonhole. At the end, trim away any loose bits of thread around the edge.

## Zippers

Don't be afraid of adding zippers! There's only one thing you may find tricky, which is that you have to sew quite near them. Once you've got over that hurdle, you'll find it easy!

If your zipper isn't the right length for your project, you can shorten a nylon zipper by sewing over it and reverse stitching back over your stitches (see page 115), going slowly over the teeth. Then trim the excess part of the zipper away.

### Using the zipper foot

The zipper foot allows the needle to sew very near the teeth of the zipper. This is because it's narrower than a general-purpose sewing machine foot, and the needle is positioned on the edge

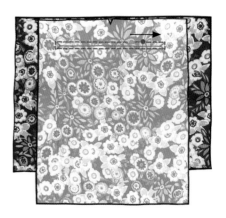

of the foot rather than in the middle. Use your sewing machine's manual to find out how to use the zipper foot on your machine. A zipper foot can also be used to sew nearer to buckles or piping.

Machines often have a quick-release button at the back of the foot holder to allow you to change the feet. To put on a new foot, lower the foot holder down onto it and click it in place. Before you sew, check that your needle won't touch the foot as it goes down. Consult your machine's manual to find out how you can move the needle position if you need to.

### Sewing a zippered letterbox internal pocket

**1** Using the template, mark the center on the wrong side of the letterbox internal pocket piece. Also transfer the thin rectangle onto the wrong side of the letterbox pocket piece, using the "pin and mark" method on the corners (see page 113). Then use a ruler and a pen or chalk marker to join up the dots to make the rectangle. Inside the rectangle, mark the central line and "V" shapes at each end. Position the letterbox internal pocket on

top of a lining piece with the right sides of the fabrics together. Match up their central notches and place the top of the pocket level with the top of the bag lining.

**2** Pin the pocket in place. Starting on a long side and with a smaller stitch (2 on the stitch dial), sew on the drawn line of the rectangle, overlapping your stitches by ⅜in (1cm) when you get round to the beginning (see page 115).

**3** Cut through the central line and the "V"s. Use smaller scissors or a seam ripper to make a hole to get you started, and cut as close to the stitches in the corners as you can without cutting through them.

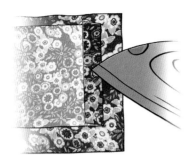

**4** Press the stitches to set them into the fabric (see page 117) as they are, but also lift up each side of the pocket and press the stitches underneath as well.

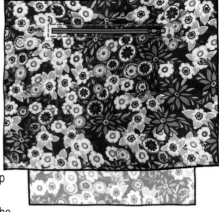

**5** "Post" the pocket piece through the letterbox opening to the wrong side and press it again, making sure the lining isn't showing on the right side. Pull the fabric taut a little at the corners so they can be pressed flat. The corners won't lie flat if you haven't snipped right into the corners, so you can go back and do that again if necessary but be careful with your scissors—one tiny snip may be just enough. Place the zipper underneath the pocket piece so that the right size of the zipper shows through the opening and is central. Fix the zipper in place by hand-bastinc (tacking) it (see page 125), gluing it using a water-soluble fabric gluestick, or by using double-sided sticky tape (washaway quilter's tape is good). Once your zipper is fixed in the opening, sew all the way around it near to the edge of the opening using a zipper foot on your sewing machine (see opposite). Start at the short zipper pull end and then overlap your stitches when you come round to the start. There is no guide to follow here, so you can either chalk out a line or use the side of a strip of masking tape as a guide (but try not to sew through it). As you are sewing close to the zipper, you may need to get your zipper pull out of the way. With the needle down, lift the presser foot up and then slide the zipper pull past the needle and out of the way, and then continue sewing. After you've sewed all the way round you can remove any basting stitches.

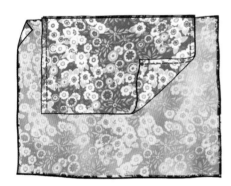

**6** From the wrong side, flip the lower half of the inner pocket upward so right sides of the letterbox pocket piece are together. Match up the raw edges at the top. Sew down both short sides of the pocket, reverse stitching at the start and finish. Sew only through the pocket piece and not through to the bag lining.

## Magnetic clasps

Another closure you can use is the magnetic clasp. It has two parts that interlink and they need to be attached before the project has been sewn so their wrong sides are hidden.

**1** Iron a small square of interfacing or fusible fleece onto the wrong side of the fabric to reinforce where the clasp will go. This will prevent the fabric ripping when the clasp is pulled (see the Glasses/Phone Case on page 72).

**2** Place the round guard disc that comes with the magnetic clasp onto the right side of the fabric. Using a pen or chalk marker, draw through the two small slits on the guard disc onto the fabric, to mark where you want your clasp to go. Use a seam ripper to cut open the slits.

**3** Insert the prongs of the clasp into the two slits from the right side of the fabric. Place the guard disc over the two prongs on the wrong side of the fabric, and fold the two prongs over the disc, toward the outside, so they are flat. A small screwdriver may help you to flatten the prongs. Follow the project instructions to attach the other side of the clasp in the same way.

# Templates

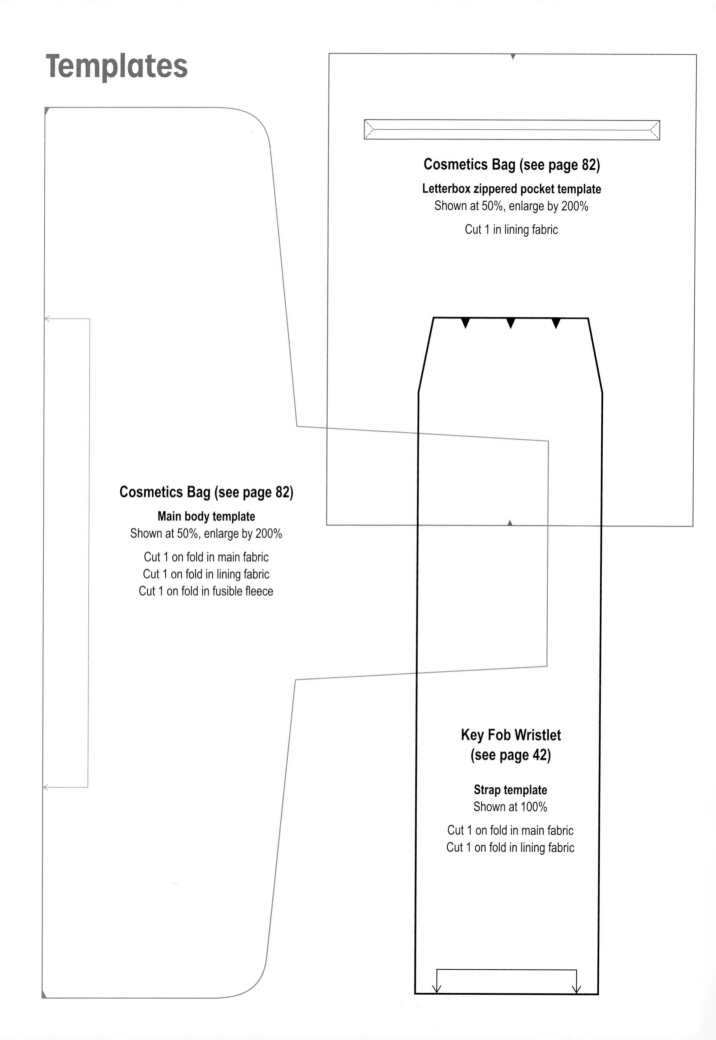

**Cosmetics Bag (see page 82)**

Letterbox zippered pocket template
Shown at 50%, enlarge by 200%

Cut 1 in lining fabric

**Cosmetics Bag (see page 82)**

**Main body template**
Shown at 50%, enlarge by 200%

Cut 1 on fold in main fabric
Cut 1 on fold in lining fabric
Cut 1 on fold in fusible fleece

**Key Fob Wristlet
(see page 42)**

**Strap template**
Shown at 100%

Cut 1 on fold in main fabric
Cut 1 on fold in lining fabric

## Regular Neck Tie (see page 54)

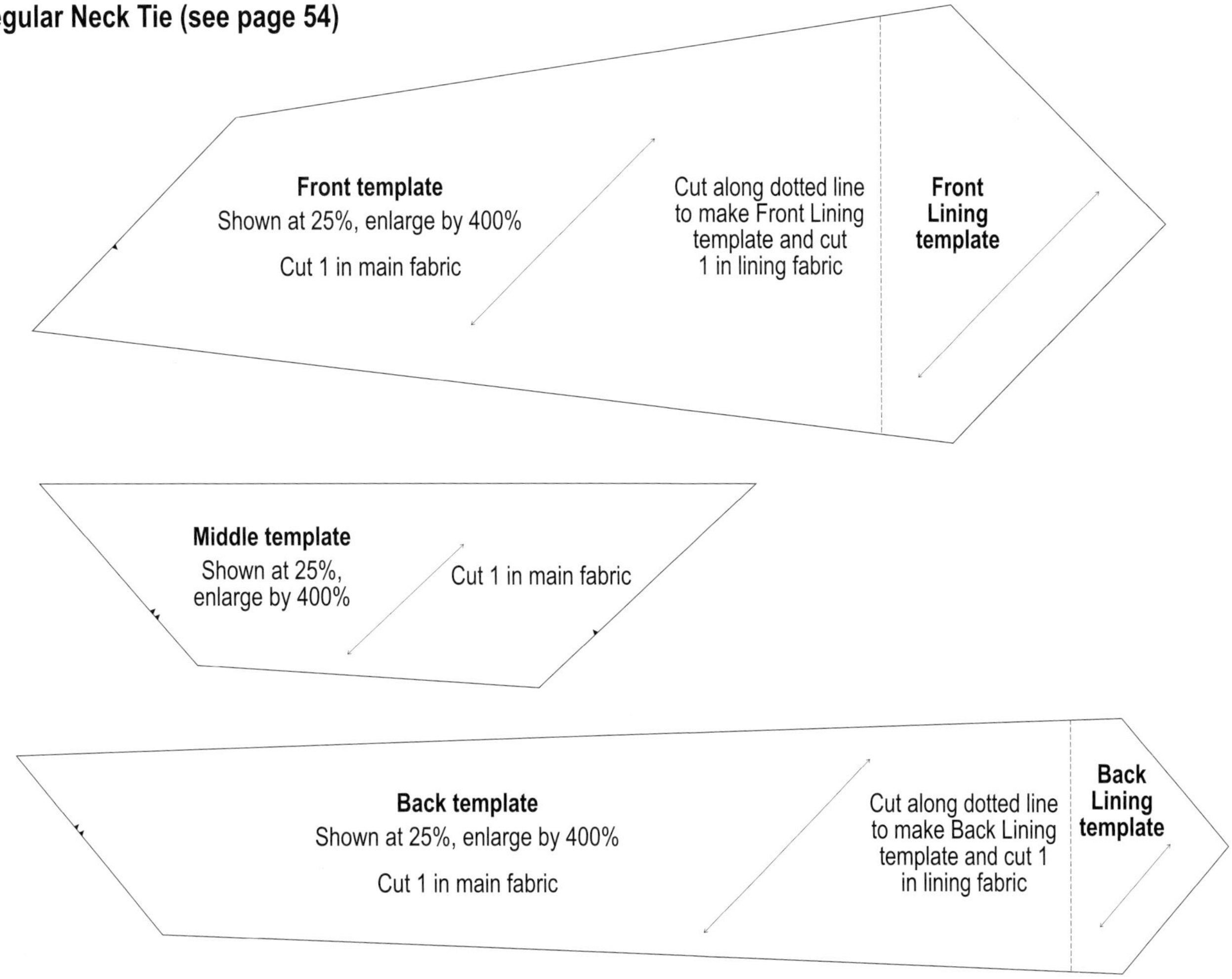

**Front template**
Shown at 25%, enlarge by 400%
Cut 1 in main fabric

Cut along dotted line to make Front Lining template and cut 1 in lining fabric

**Front Lining template**

**Middle template**
Shown at 25%, enlarge by 400%

Cut 1 in main fabric

**Back template**
Shown at 25%, enlarge by 400%
Cut 1 in main fabric

Cut along dotted line to make Back Lining template and cut 1 in lining fabric

**Back Lining template**

## Skinny Neck Tie (see page 54)

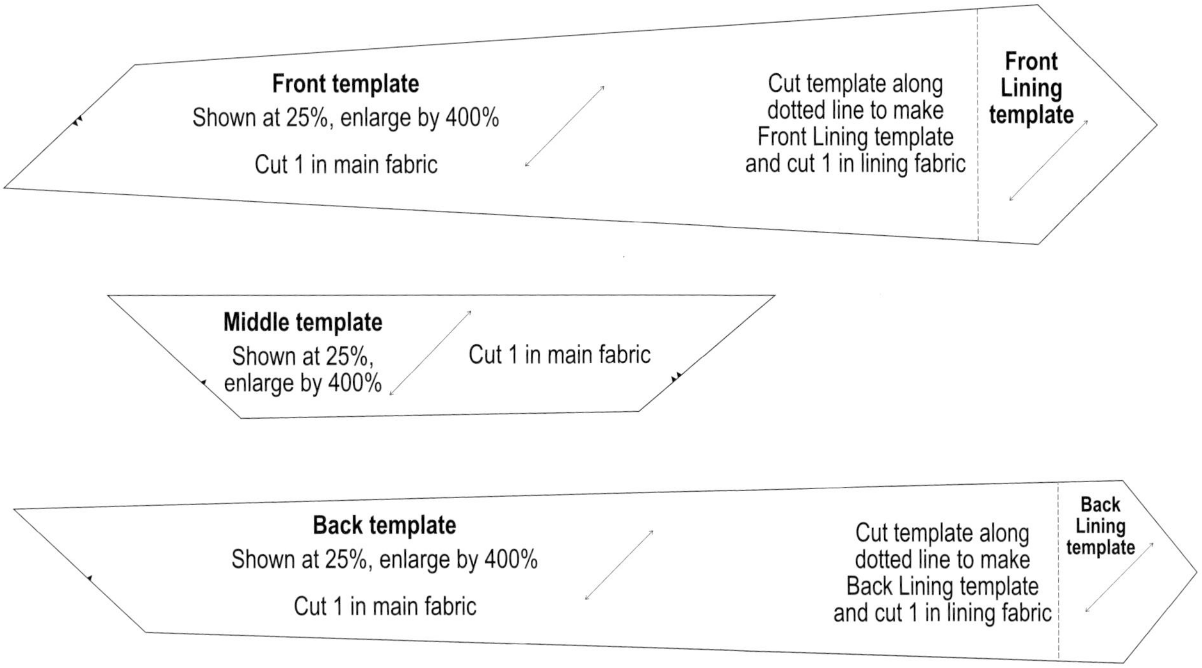

**Front template**
Shown at 25%, enlarge by 400%
Cut 1 in main fabric

Cut template along dotted line to make Front Lining template and cut 1 in lining fabric

**Front Lining template**

**Middle template**
Shown at 25%, enlarge by 400%

Cut 1 in main fabric

**Back template**
Shown at 25%, enlarge by 400%
Cut 1 in main fabric

Cut template along dotted line to make Back Lining template and cut 1 in lining fabric

**Back Lining template**

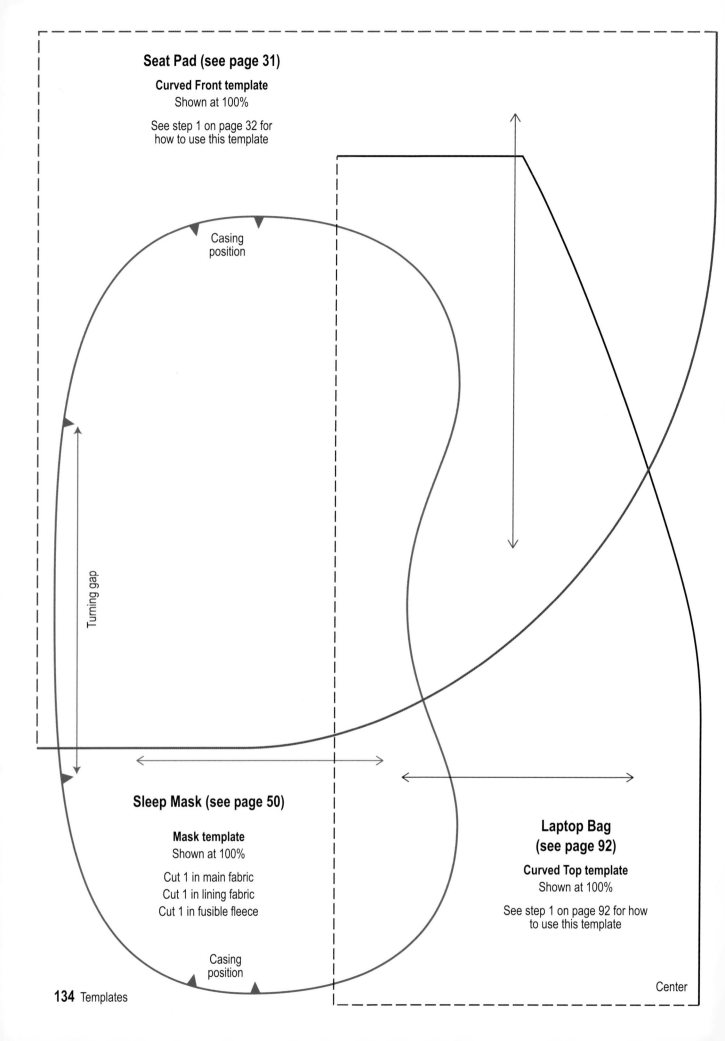

**Seat Pad (see page 31)**

**Curved Front template**
Shown at 100%

See step 1 on page 32 for
how to use this template

Casing
position

Turning gap

**Sleep Mask (see page 50)**

**Mask template**
Shown at 100%

Cut 1 in main fabric
Cut 1 in lining fabric
Cut 1 in fusible fleece

Casing
position

**Laptop Bag
(see page 92)**

**Curved Top template**
Shown at 100%

See step 1 on page 92 for how
to use this template

Center

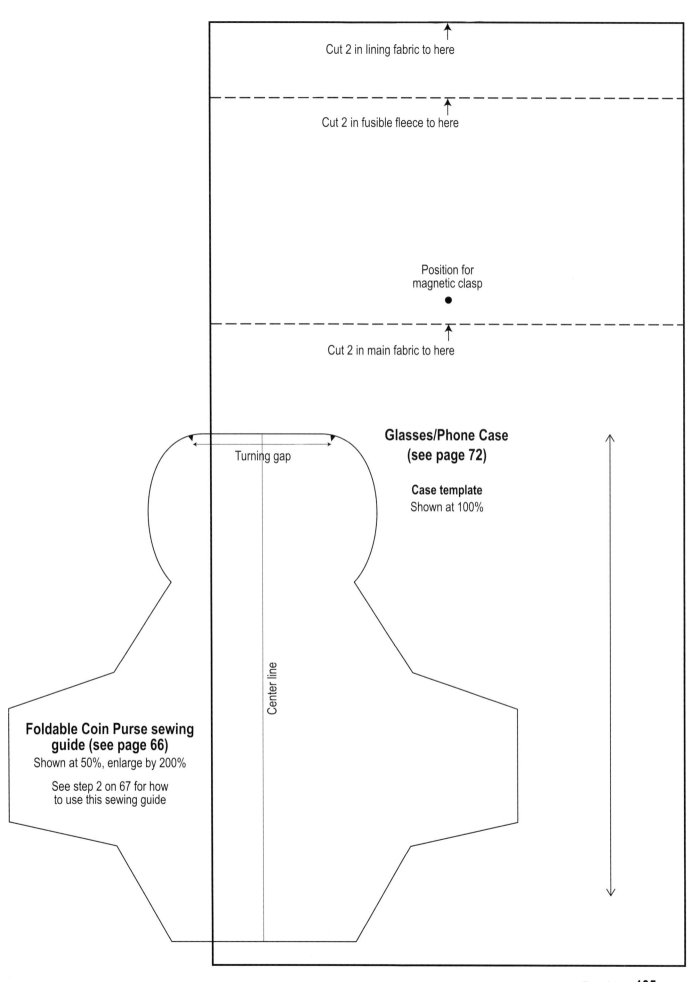

Cut 2 in lining fabric to here

Cut 2 in fusible fleece to here

Position for
magnetic clasp

Cut 2 in main fabric to here

Turning gap

**Glasses/Phone Case
(see page 72)**

**Case template**
Shown at 100%

Center line

**Foldable Coin Purse sewing
guide (see page 66)**
Shown at 50%, enlarge by 200%

See step 2 on 67 for how
to use this sewing guide

## Pet Bed diagram (see page 22)

Use the measurements on this diagram
to draft out the template at 100% (see page 112)

Cut 1 on fold in fleece fabric

35½in (90cm)

22½in (57cm)

6¼in (16cm)

6¼in (16cm)

6¼in (16cm)

6¼in (16cm)

22¾in (58cm)

2¾in (7cm)

19⅝in (50cm)

2¾in (7cm)

## Reversible Tote Bag diagram (see page 60)

Use the measurements on
this diagram to draft out the
template at 100%. Also see the
instructions on the right.

Cut 2 in fabric A
Cut 2 in fabric B

19⅝in (50cm)

3⅛in (8cm)

3⅛in (8cm)

3⅛in (8cm)

3⅛in (8cm)

2¾in (7cm)

2¾in (7cm)

7½in (19cm)

7½in (19cm)

To draft out the Reversible Tote
Bag template:

1) Draw and cut out a 19⅝ x 19⅝in
(50 x 50cm) square. Fold it in
half to find the center and mark
the center at the top and bottom
edges.

2) Mark 2¾in (7cm) in from the top
left-hand side and top right-hand
side for the strap positions.

3) Along the bottom edge,
measure and mark 7½in (19cm)
from the center on both sides.
Draw a line from the top corners
down to these marks. Also from
these marks, mark 2¾in (7cm) in
toward the center, 3⅛in (8cm) up
and 3⅛in (8cm) across to meet
each side of the bag as indicated.
This will create the boxed corners
of your bag.

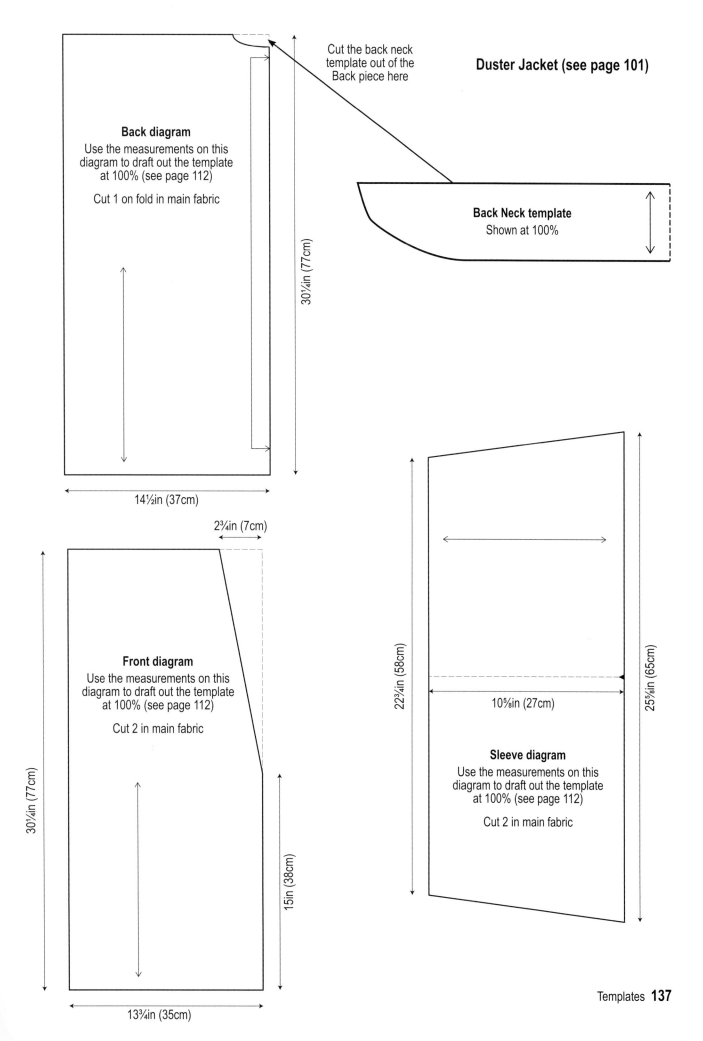

Cut the back neck template out of the Back piece here

**Duster Jacket (see page 101)**

**Back Neck template**
Shown at 100%

**Back diagram**
Use the measurements on this diagram to draft out the template at 100% (see page 112)

Cut 1 on fold in main fabric

30¼in (77cm)

14½in (37cm)

2¾in (7cm)

**Front diagram**
Use the measurements on this diagram to draft out the template at 100% (see page 112)

Cut 2 in main fabric

30¼in (77cm)

15in (38cm)

13¾in (35cm)

22¾in (58cm)

10⅝in (27cm)

25⅝in (65cm)

**Sleeve diagram**
Use the measurements on this diagram to draft out the template at 100% (see page 112)

Cut 2 in main fabric

# French Press Jacket
(see page 34)

**Large French Press Jacket (8 cup/1 liter) sewing guide**

Shown at 50%, enlarge by 200%

See step 2 on page 34 for how to use this sewing guide

**Small French Press Jacket (2 cup/0.4 liter) sewing guide**

Shown at 50%, enlarge by 200%

See step 2 on page 34 for how to use this sewing guide

# Bucket Hat (see page 57)

**Brim template**

Shown at 50%, enlarge by 200%

Cut 4 in main fabric

**Crown template**

Shown at 50%, enlarge by 200%

Cut 1 in main fabric
Cut 1 in lining fabric

**Side template**

Shown at 50%, enlarge by 200%

Cut 1 on fold in main fabric
Cut 1 on fold in lining fabric

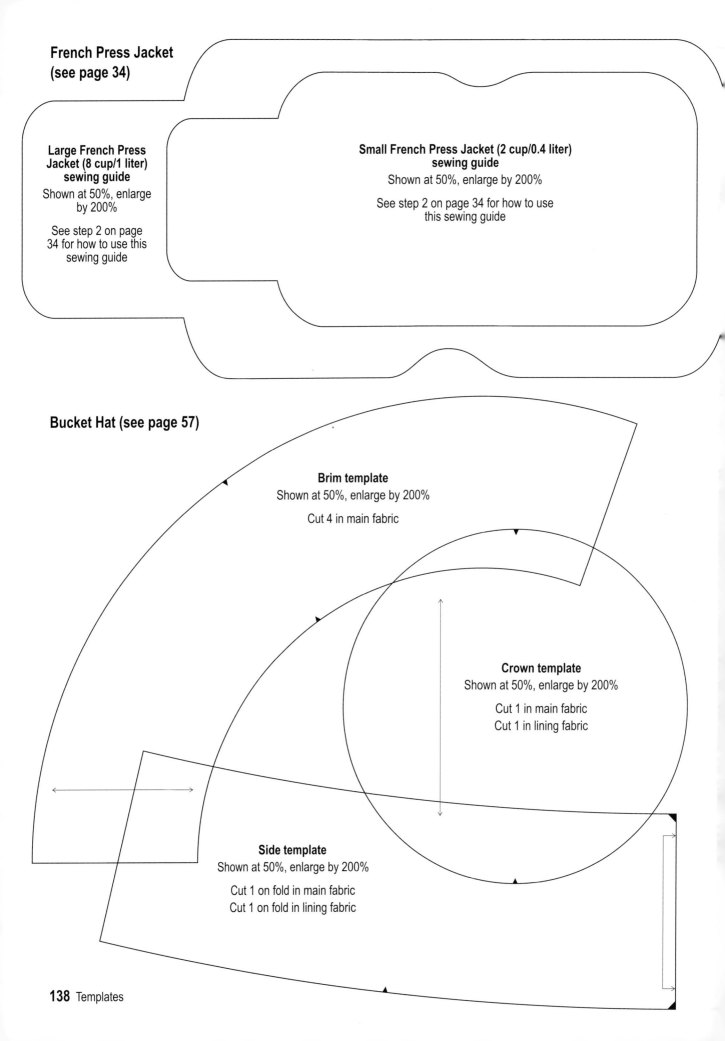

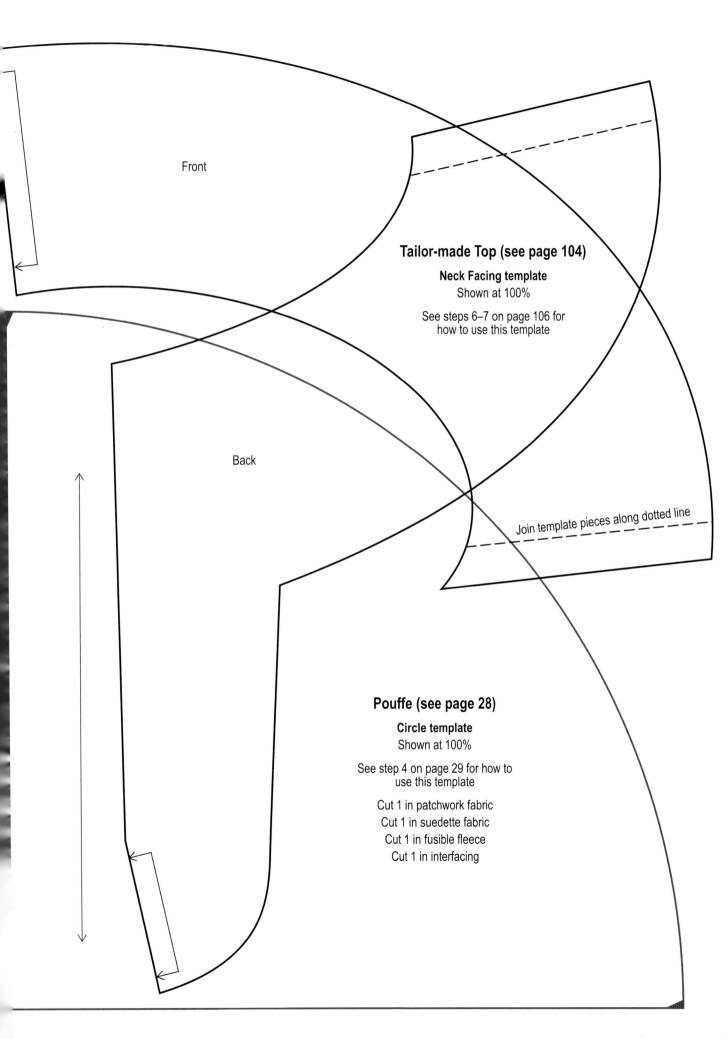

Front

**Tailor-made Top (see page 104)**

**Neck Facing template**
Shown at 100%

See steps 6–7 on page 106 for
how to use this template

Back

Join template pieces along dotted line

**Pouffe (see page 28)**

**Circle template**
Shown at 100%

See step 4 on page 29 for how to
use this template

Cut 1 in patchwork fabric
Cut 1 in suedette fabric
Cut 1 in fusible fleece
Cut 1 in interfacing

# Soft Plant Pot Covers (see page 19)

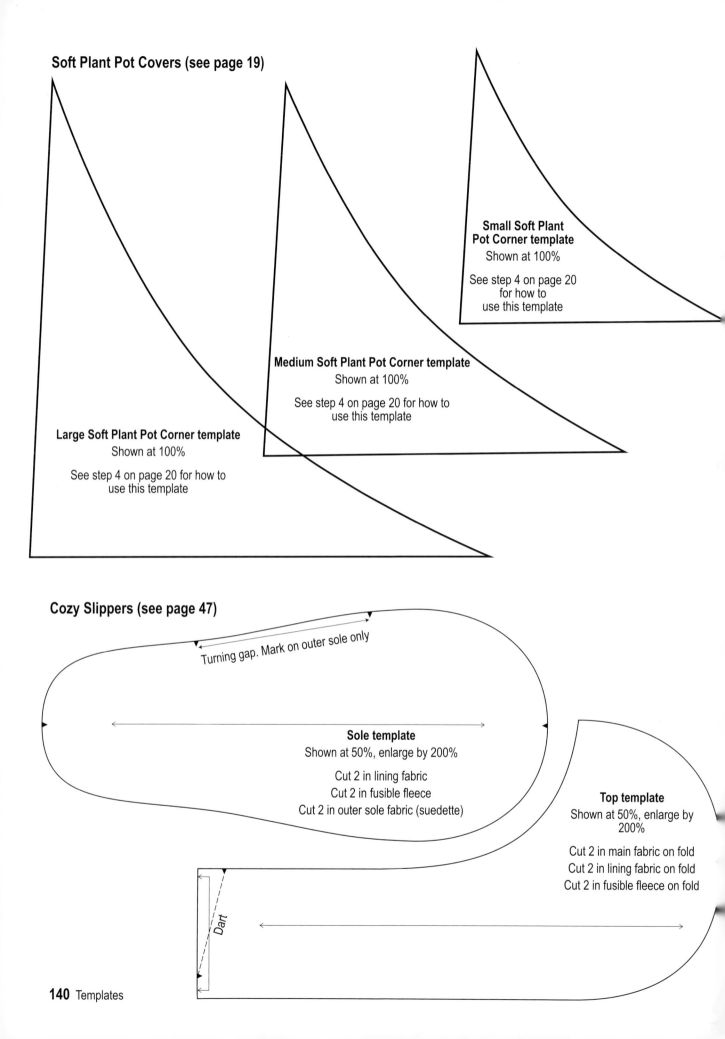

**Small Soft Plant Pot Corner template**
Shown at 100%

See step 4 on page 20
for how to
use this template

**Medium Soft Plant Pot Corner template**
Shown at 100%

See step 4 on page 20 for how to
use this template

**Large Soft Plant Pot Corner template**
Shown at 100%

See step 4 on page 20 for how to
use this template

# Cozy Slippers (see page 47)

Turning gap. Mark on outer sole only

**Sole template**
Shown at 50%, enlarge by 200%

Cut 2 in lining fabric
Cut 2 in fusible fleece
Cut 2 in outer sole fabric (suedette)

**Top template**
Shown at 50%, enlarge by
200%

Cut 2 in main fabric on fold
Cut 2 in lining fabric on fold
Cut 2 in fusible fleece on fold

Dart

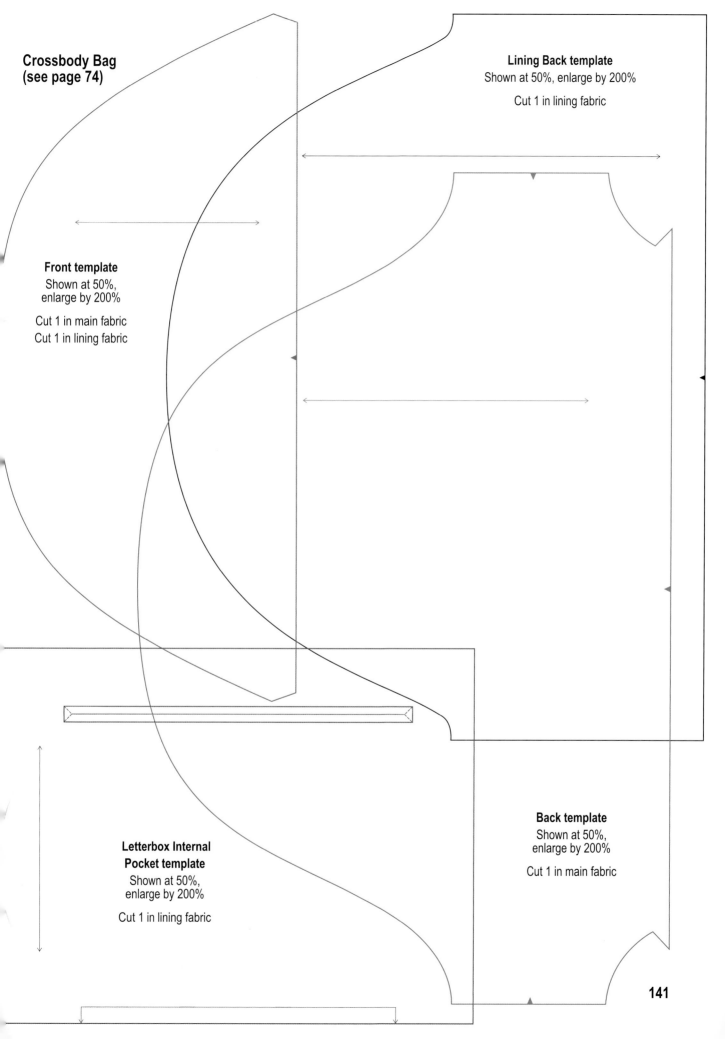

**Crossbody Bag
(see page 74)**

**Lining Back template**
Shown at 50%, enlarge by 200%

Cut 1 in lining fabric

**Front template**
Shown at 50%,
enlarge by 200%

Cut 1 in main fabric
Cut 1 in lining fabric

**Back template**
Shown at 50%,
enlarge by 200%

Cut 1 in main fabric

**Letterbox Internal
Pocket template**
Shown at 50%,
enlarge by 200%

Cut 1 in lining fabric

141

## Plush Tote (see page 78)

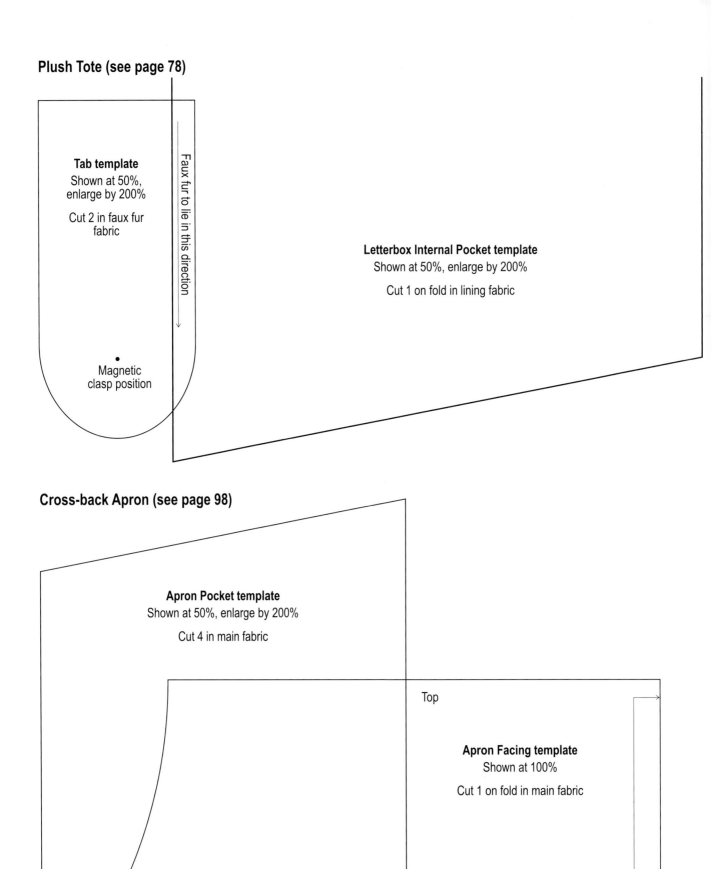

**Tab template**
Shown at 50%, enlarge by 200%

Cut 2 in faux fur fabric

Faux fur to lie in this direction

• Magnetic clasp position

**Letterbox Internal Pocket template**
Shown at 50%, enlarge by 200%

Cut 1 on fold in lining fabric

## Cross-back Apron (see page 98)

**Apron Pocket template**
Shown at 50%, enlarge by 200%

Cut 4 in main fabric

Top

**Apron Facing template**
Shown at 100%

Cut 1 on fold in main fabric

Turning gap

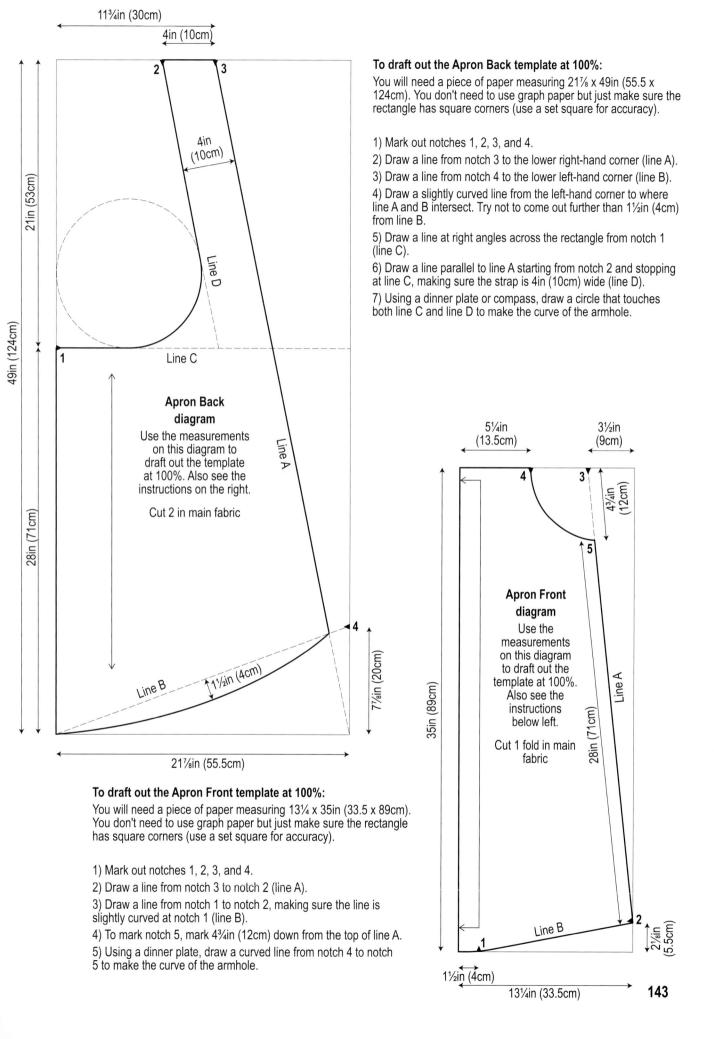

11¾in (30cm)

4in (10cm)

4in (10cm)

21in (53cm)

49in (124cm)

28in (71cm)

2

3

1

Line D

Line C

Line A

**Apron Back diagram**

Use the measurements on this diagram to draft out the template at 100%. Also see the instructions on the right.

Cut 2 in main fabric

Line B

1½in (4cm)

4

7⅞in (20cm)

21⅞in (55.5cm)

**To draft out the Apron Back template at 100%:**

You will need a piece of paper measuring 21⅞ x 49in (55.5 x 124cm). You don't need to use graph paper but just make sure the rectangle has square corners (use a set square for accuracy).

1) Mark out notches 1, 2, 3, and 4.

2) Draw a line from notch 3 to the lower right-hand corner (line A).

3) Draw a line from notch 4 to the lower left-hand corner (line B).

4) Draw a slightly curved line from the left-hand corner to where line A and B intersect. Try not to come out further than 1½in (4cm) from line B.

5) Draw a line at right angles across the rectangle from notch 1 (line C).

6) Draw a line parallel to line A starting from notch 2 and stopping at line C, making sure the strap is 4in (10cm) wide (line D).

7) Using a dinner plate or compass, draw a circle that touches both line C and line D to make the curve of the armhole.

5¼in (13.5cm)

3½in (9cm)

4

3

4¾in (12cm)

5

**Apron Front diagram**

Use the measurements on this diagram to draft out the template at 100%. Also see the instructions below left.

Cut 1 fold in main fabric

35in (89cm)

28in (71cm)

Line A

Line B

1

2

2⅛in (5.5cm)

1½in (4cm)

13¼in (33.5cm)

**To draft out the Apron Front template at 100%:**

You will need a piece of paper measuring 13¼ x 35in (33.5 x 89cm). You don't need to use graph paper but just make sure the rectangle has square corners (use a set square for accuracy).

1) Mark out notches 1, 2, 3, and 4.

2) Draw a line from notch 3 to notch 2 (line A).

3) Draw a line from notch 1 to notch 2, making sure the line is slightly curved at notch 1 (line B).

4) To mark notch 5, mark 4¾in (12cm) down from the top of line A.

5) Using a dinner plate, draw a curved line from notch 4 to notch 5 to make the curve of the armhole.

# Index

Apron, Cross-back 98–100

bags and purses
  Bag Organizer 88–91
  Bag Strap 64–65
  bag-making skills and fastenings
    128–131
  Cosmetics Bag 82–87
  Crossbody Bag 74–77
  Foldable Coin Purse 66–68
  Foldaway Tote 69–71
  Glasses/Phone Case 72–73
  Laptop Bag 92–95
  Plush Tote 78–81
  Reversible Tote Bag 60–63
Bowl and Mug Cozies 11–13
Bucket Hat 57–59
buttons 5, 129
  buttonholes 130
  shank buttons 129

Coin Purse, Foldable 66–68
corners
  boxed 128
  clipping 119
  mitered 121
  sewing 116
Cosmetics Bag 82–87
Crossbody Bag 74–77
curves
  clipping 119
  sewing 116
cutting out and pinning 112–113

darts 121
Duster Jacket 101–103

fabrics
  choosing 5
  cutting out and pinning 112–113
  directional prints 113
  lining fabrics 5
  mark-making 113
  pressing 117
  right side/wrong side 122
  selvage 112
fastenings
  buttons 5, 129
  magnetic clasps 131
  zippers 130–131
folded straps 129
French Press Jacket 34–37
French seams 120

Garden Kneeler 26–27
Glasses/Phone Case 72–73

hand sewing 124–125
  fastening off 124
  securing your thread 124
  tacking/basting 125
  threading a needle 124
  see also stitches (hand stitches)
hems 121
  blind hemming 87

Key Fob Wristlet 42–43

Laptop Bag 92–95

Napkins 8–10
Neck Tie 54–56
needles
  sewing machine 5
  threading 124
Notebook Cover, Reversible 44–46

patch pockets 123
patchwork 126–127
Pet Bed 22–25
Pillow, Zippered 14–18
Plant Pot Covers, Soft 19–21
pockets
  letterbox internal pocket 130–131
  patch pockets 123
Pouffe 28–30
pressing 117, 120

quilting 127

scissors 5
Scrunchie 40–41
seam ripper 117
seams 118–120
  clipping corners 119
  clipping curves 119
  French seams 120
  grading (layering) 119
  matching different fabrics 120
  pressing 117, 120
  reducing bulk 119
  reinforcing 119
  seam allowances 4, 118
  setting seams 117
Seat Pad 31–33
selvage 112
sewing kit 5
sewing machine 5
  free arm sewing 115
  needles 5
  sewing skills 114–123
  using 114
  zipper foot 130
  see also stitches (machine stitches)
Skirt, Drawstring 109–111
Sleep Mask 50–53
Slippers, Cozy 47–49

stitches (hand stitches)
  ladder stitch 125
  running stitch 125
  slipstitch 125
  whipstitch 125
stitches (machine stitches)
  114–115
  handwheel stitches 115
  reverse stitch 115
  topstitch 114
  understitching 123
  undoing 117
sustainable sewing 4

Table Runner 8–10
tacking/basting 125
Tailor-made Top 104–108
templates 112, 132–143
  notches, transferring 112
  pinning to fabrics 113
threads 5
  fastening off 124
  securing 124
  tangles 125
  threading a needle 124
topstitching 5, 114
tote bags see bags and purses
tube straps 128–129
turning gaps 122–123

zippers 130–131

# Suppliers

## US

**Create for Less**
www.createforless.com

**Hobby Lobby**
www.hobbylobby.com

**Joann Fabric & Crafts**
www.joann.com

**Michaels**
www.michaels.com

## UK

**Ditto Fabrics**
www.dittofabrics.co.uk

**Fabrics galore**
www.fabricsgalore.co.uk

**Higgs and Higgs**
www.higgsandhiggs.com

**Hobbycraft**
www.hobbycraft.co.uk

# Acknowledgments

I would like to thank the numerous students I have taught how to sew (probably in the thousands by now!). They have been the inspiration for this book and have made me a better teacher.

I'm so grateful to CICO Books for giving me the opportunity to write this, my second book, about a subject I am so passionate about. I would like to thank Cindy Richards, Penny Craig, Carmel Edmonds, Alison Fenton, Sally Powell, James Gardiner, Nel Haynes, and Gordana Simakovic.

A special thank you goes out to Jenny Dye, my editor. We've worked hard and long over the past few months and her help has been invaluable. Thank you also to illustrator Cathy Brear who brought my hundreds of photos (my phone is bursting at the seams!) to life with her amazing and detailed illustrations.